PUPPY TRAINING – START TODAY!

Mold Your Puppy

Into a Great Dog!

By Ted Baer

About the Author

Ted Baer made a significant impact in the motion picture industry during the 1980s with his exceptional dog, Tundra. Thanks to Ted's groundbreaking training techniques, Tundra mastered over 200-word commands and more than 70 hand signals. Tundra's remarkable abilities earned her the coveted PATSY Award, the highest honor for a performing animal, for her debut national performance in a ninety-minute special of "The Love Boat." This award is bestowed upon only one dog actor each year. Tundra's career in Hollywood skyrocketed, leading to roles in four movies and over eighty television appearances, solidifying her status as a legendary canine star.

Ted Baer's first book, *"Communicating With Your Dog,"* not only won a prestigious Dog Writer's Association of America Award but also went on to sell over 200,000 copies. His groundbreaking work significantly advanced dog training in America, shaping the practices of future trainers. As one of the pioneering figures in dog training, Ted recognized that dogs are eager to listen to us, but it is up to us to bridge the communication gap. His contributions have left an indelible mark on the field, making him a revered authority in canine training.

Check out *"Communicating With Your Dog"* and Ted's book, *"That's Cool!"*, both available on Amazon. *"That's Cool!"* teaches 49 awesome tricks and skills to raise your cool factor.

Introduction

I created a straightforward communication system that can be used with any puppy or dog. This system allowed me to teach my dog, Tundra, an extensive vocabulary of commands, enabling her to perform extraordinary behaviors.

This book introduces a simple communication system for you to use with your puppy. It's designed to be both easy and enjoyable. Start your puppy out on the right paw!

The need for a communication system for dogs has been long overdue. Throughout history, humans have developed complex languages to communicate with each other and even with machines, often with dogs by their side. Different breeds were utilized for their unique skills in herding, guarding, hunting, sled pulling, and even rescuing, helping humans achieve their goals. Despite the obvious need, no simple and logical language for dogs had been developed.

In this book, you'll learn to communicate with your puppy using an easy-to-learn twenty-word language, along with simple training skills to teach this language to your puppy. This foundation will lead to further training and a deeper bond of friendship and understanding between you and your furry friend.

#1 Communication by Means of a Language

Dogs can be proud of the old adage associated with them. The phrase "man's best friend" tells us a lot about the history of dogs and their basic nature. I cannot think of a better compliment or truer characterization of dogs in general.

Fido's only aim is to please you. You are the highlight of his life. He studies you and depends on you for his food, water, and shelter. He recognizes how you hold your body when you're happy, angry, nervous, or tired. He can even sense your deep feelings. Gradually, Fido will adopt your character, personality, and some believe, even your looks.

The next time you find yourself in a bad mood, observe the way your dog behaves. The typical dog senses your mood and, with ears back, will approach you submissively, as if to apologize for not pleasing you.

Dogs are loyal companions whose lack of understanding is not their fault. Relatively few dogs who get scolded or punished ever know why. Dogs need to be disciplined in a way that enables them to understand what they did wrong. If Fido doesn't do what he's told, chances are that you are at fault.

To give your puppy a chance to please you, it is necessary that you use a system of communication that is simple and clear. Though people possess intelligence, reason, logic, and, for the most part, wisdom, they speak to their puppies and dogs in a confusing and illogical way.

The widely used commands, "Sit down!" and "Lie down!" are good examples of this. Notice that both commands use two words when only one is necessary. Also, in each of the commands you find the word "down." Does the confusion end here? Not quite. When using the "lie down" command, people often interchange "lie" and "lay." Fido's life would be much simpler if "sit" were used for sitting and "down" for lying down.

Fido will often carry out a master's command, but not because the command is stated correctly. Take the case when the resident chef catches his or her best friend in the kitchen trying to make off with the family's lamb chops and yells, "You rotten dog! Get out of here!" Fido makes tracks and hides for a while--not because he understands the words of the command, but because he senses his master's displeasure.

The best dog trainers in the world have said that a dog is capable of learning as many as one hundred verbal commands in a lifetime. My star pupil, Tundra, knew more than two hundred verbal commands and more than seventy hand signals. Tundra's vocabulary grew to this level quickly and formed a very solid base. With this base I was able to communicate any action to her verbally. New words were added only occasionally, when needed.

Regarding Tundra's training, I would like to point out that her knowledge increased at an accelerating rate. In other words, as Tundra's knowledge developed, things came to her more quickly and easily. Few researchers have been concerned with the rate at which a dog learns. But it seems logical that it would be much easier for Tundra to relate any new training to that which she already knew and understood - - and so it was. Based on my experience, I do not believe there is a saturation point in a dog's learning ability.

The special language found in this book will allow your puppy to grow in its ability to understand communications. You will be given twenty words, and, with consistent use and reinforcement, your pet will develop a "vocabulary," much as a young child does. The consistency in using the same words, the same method of speaking, and the same logical order will avoid confusion. Your success at using this language will determine your puppy's success in understanding your wishes.

Originally, when teaching Tundra, the word "growl," a

problem arose because its sound was too close to the command "howl." The word command "growl" was changed to "scare," and I no longer confused her. To avoid this kind of confusion and to make it easier for your puppy, the "magic" words used in this book are one-syllable words, each with its own separate and identifiable sound.

It's a wonderful feeling owning a puppy that listens to you. You'll find that the twenty-word language will give you a solid base for communication. Your puppy will be a happy puppy. It will not only know when it has been bad or good, but it will understand your wishes and be able to please you more. Because of its new knowledge, you'll be more likely to take your best friend with you wherever you go. So please be selfish and spoil yourself. Spend a little time with your puppy. It's the only investment that I know of that returns a hundredfold.

#2 Family Cooperation

It is extremely important that you have your family's cooperation in carrying out the program presented in this book. Review the material and practice it daily with your **puppy**. Make sure that your family understands what you are trying to do and is willing to help. Assure them that the program is simple and easy if carried outproperly. Explain to them the value of having a **puppy** that follows simple commands.

When I say "family," I mean everyone who comes in contact with your **puppy** in your house. That includes all members of the household and frequent visitors - - at least those visitors who like to talk and play with your **puppy**.

It will be easy to gain your family's cooperation if you go about it in the right way. Start by arousing their interest. Pick a time to introduce and discuss the program when the family normally gathers. You can't expect them all to take the time to read this book. Tell them the purpose of a special dog language. Stress how easy it will be for them to learn twenty words in particular sequences.

Next, discuss each of the rules found in Chapter 4. As you bring up each one, allow your family to discuss what it means and why it is important. Make certain that they understand each of the rules.

Finally, introduce the first nine words of the language to your family. These words will be found in Chapters 5, 6, 7, and 8. Go over each individually. Explain the word's meaning and talk about its uses. Members of the family will be allowed to use only these nine words when talking to your **puppy**.

Included in this chapter, you will find an outline that you may want to **follow at your family meeting. It contains the list** of rules and commands that you will want to post for them. Place them where they can be referred to easily. If there are children in the family, you will want to post the rules and commands where they won't need an extension ladder to read them.

You must be a firm leader. The whole ball game depends upon you. You are the coach of your team, the captain, the umpire, the cheerleader, as well as one of the players.

As the coach it is up to you to review periodically the rules of the game with the team. As you introduce each new word, you must tell team members how you taught it and when it can be used.

As the captain you will inspire your teammates, you won't let them become discouraged, and you will keep them all working together. You will be the one calling the plays.

As the umpire you will correct any player who fails to follow the rules. Mistakes are inevitable. Catch them and correct them immediately. In doing this, I strongly recommend that you use a code word like "gumball" to let a player know that he or she has committed an error. As umpire it is up to you to see that no member of the team changes, repeats, or countermands another teammate's command. I will warn you about these things again in Chapter 4, and I'll tell you why they are mistakes.

As cheerleader you will keep the team enthusiastic. You have a product to get them excited about - - Twenty Magic Words! Encourage your teammates when they need it. Support them in every way possible as they learn to communicate with their little mascot!

Always remember that you play the most important role in the game. The game is literally in your hands. Everything depends upon you. You will have to determine when the additional words will be introduced to your family. As with the initial words, you should teach them to your **puppy** first. Chapter 10 has special commands that can be extremely helpful to the family. Review your family's progress and introduce new words at any convenient family gathering.

The benefits of the training program go far beyond the development of a lovable, obedient dog that truly can become a welcomed member of the family. You and the other members will become conscious of communication skills that you can apply not only to your dog but to little children and people in general. And the fact that you are working together on the project will bring you all closer together as a family.

Meeting Outline

The Purpose of a Special Dog Language

1. Effective communication makes life easier for your dog and makes him or her happy and obedient.
2. The twenty-word language is simple and logical for your dog.
3. Anything else is confusing.
4. Consistent use of the words avoids confusion.
5. Lack of understanding is not your dog's fault.
6. The family will find it simple, beneficial, educational, and fun.

The Rules

1. Be consistent.
2. Work as a family unit.
3. Match voice tone to command.
4. Exercise patience.
5. Think like a dog.
6. Respect your dog as a "person".
7. Praise rather than punish.
8. Praise or correct immediately.
9. Ask only the possible.
10. Give a command only once.
11. Release each command.
12. Allow your dog to be good.
13. Train before dinner.
14. Play after other training sessions.
15. Record your dog's progress.

The First Nine Words

1. Your dog's name
2. *Good*
3. *Bad*
4. *No*
5. *Stay*
6. *Go*
7. *Come*
8. *Sit*
9. *Down*

Other Information

1. Only the nine words may be used by others.
2. Use an inoffensive word to reprimand a violator.
3. Respect each other's commands.

#3 Communication Bell

Domesticated dogs have four major needs: food, water, expulsion of waste, and affection. Dogs have always struggled to communicate these needs.

When Fido is hungry, he might be extremely friendly or look at you with a pair of sad eyes. When he's thirty, he might make gestures toward the kitchen sink to get your attention, or even run around to the bathrooms to see if anyone left the lid of the toilet up. When he needs a walk to urinate or defecate, he will try anything from crying at the door to jumping up and down excitedly. As for affection, every owner knows the cute things that a dog will do to get some loving.

Of the four major needs, there are two, water and expulsion of waste, that Fido can easily warn you about. I credit a classmate, Chris Pond, for the following idea he gave me in the 70's. Chris's mother had a cat that used to play with her wind chimes. The cat would use the chimes to gain her attention when she wanted to go outside. When Chris got a **puppy**, he started teaching him to play with the chimes. He said it came naturally to the **puppy** after watching the cat do it many times. This idea deserves our attention and applause!

To begin using this idea in your own home, you need a bell. Any bell will work. If you have two dogs and one is small and the other large, choose a multiple bell design. Here the difference in size won't hinder the dogs from nudging the bell. Just hang the bell from your doorknob with strong cord or maybe a leather strap. Hang another bell by your dog's water dish. Each dog will choose to nudge it differently. Tundra would nose it, while another member of our canine family developed her own technique. She brushes against it with her body. One bell should be placed at the door where the dog normally leaves to go outside and another where he receives his

11

water.

Training your **puppy** to use the bell is an easy process. The secret is to be consistent! Every time Fido goes through the door for a walk, make him nudge the bell first. If he is standing over an empty water dish (heaven knows it was unintentional!) looking up for water, help him nudge the bell, and then give him the water.

To get your **puppy** to nudge the bell, always use the same words: *nose* it. (see Chapter 9). Bring Fido's nose over to the bell and help him to push it. When he finally sounds the bell, offer praise. Immediately take him for a walk or give him the water he wants. Refrain from ever giving your **puppy** food for

pushing the bell. Though food makes an excellent reward, it will always stick in the **puppy's** mind that the bell means food. Be patient. The ten seconds that you devote to the bell four times a day will produce the results you want. Fido might take from one week to two months to understand the bell, but then the bell will be part of his life.

If you find that your **puppy** shies away from the bell, rub a favorite odor on it or tape a piece of food to it. Try a piece of roast beef. I guarantee that your **puppy** will then be interested and will get close enough to it to nudge it with your help.

For the sake of your door, never allow Fido to paw the bell. The nails of his paws will not only scratch the door, but any other door in the house will also fall victim when Fido wants to get through. If you see Fido attempting to paw the bell, run over quickly, give him one squirt from a squirt bottle filled with water, and tell him sternly that he's bad (see Chapter 6). Then get to a positive note. Quickly help him to nose the bell and give the just reward he deserves - - water or a walk.

It will be a happy day the first time that Fido needs a walk and rings the bell on his own. Be sure to respond with praise, and then go for a walk immediately. Once your puppy has mastered the communication bell, praise will no longer be necessary. Your puppy will understand which bell to nose to get the message across, thus satisfying its need.

#4 The Rules

This chapter discusses the rules that you and your family should follow in teaching your puppy the Twenty Magic Words. The rules set forth a basic guide to having an obedient puppy. Review these rules occasionally to evaluate your progress. Any violation of these rules will hamper your progress with your puppy.

Rule 1: Be Consistent

It is important that you be consistent in the use of the language. The puppy who responds to "Fang, come!" will surely be confused if you say, "Get over here!" If you are using the wrong word to represent a particular action, the puppy can't second guess you. Use only the language outlined in this book.

You also must be consistent in your training methods. A consistent and proper correction is essential! If you are busy watching television and allow your puppy to get away with something bad, your puppy will certainly test you further. Often a person makes the mistake of praising a puppy for incorrect behavior. An example of this is when Duchess jumps up on her owner. The owner's natural response is to pet the puppy. In so doing, he or she rewards the puppy for doing something objectionable. Another good example is when Duchess is barking in the backyard - - something puppies often do to gain attention. Not wanting to catch grief from the neighbors, the owner runs to the back door and offers her a silencing chew toy or even lets her come into the house. By rewarding the puppy for barking, the owner simply defeats his or her own purpose. Such mistakes can make you your puppy's pet.

Rule 2: Work as a Family Unit

The ideal way to train Duchess is to live alone with her. In general, the more people living with your puppy, the harder it will be for you to train her. The only exception to this is when a family is operating as a unit. The whole family must participate in your puppy's language, discipline, rules, and, most importantly, her praise!

You have the responsibility of teaching your family the language and the rules. In Chapter 2, I discussed the need for family unity in training your puppy. Before you begin teaching anyone else, however, be sure you have read this book from cover to cover and that you have a firm grasp of the material contained in the more pertinent sections.

Rule 3: Match Voice Tone to Command

Puppies rely on the tone of a person's voice. It is an easy guide they learn at an early age. A person's tone varies when he or she is angry, sad, happy, confused, or anxious. This acquired knowledge that your puppy has learned can be helpful during training. Your tone should be in keeping with the nature of the command. In general, a command should sound serious. Your puppy will be more likely to respect a command if it is given in a way that sounds important and urgent. *Good, bad,* and *no* (Chapter 6) need special attention given to the tone. These words are feedback words for your puppy. Let Duchess feel from your tone whether she's been good or bad. On certain commands, an excited tone will stimulate excitement in your puppy. Play this by ear and watch for the reaction.

Volume is another variable in your voice that must be considered. I recommend a normal volume with the emphasis on tone. If your puppy is some distance away, it will be necessary to increase your volume accordingly. Also, when you are upset with your puppy, it is a good release of tension to say *"Bad!"* using a higher volume. Warning! Rumors may fly around your neighborhood as to your mental stability. Yell at your own risk!

During your training sessions, when your puppy's

attention is focused on you, it is a good idea to practice volume reduction. By giving your commands in a whisper, you will teach your puppy to listen to you more closely.

Rule 4: Exercise Patience

We all have patience to a greater or lesser degree. The more you have, the more success you'll have in training your puppy. Some people with little patience may still be successful with their puppies because of their great love for the four-legged beasties! When their patience runs out, these people should retreat, calm down, and then try again!

People say that I am very patient. It's easy for me to be patient around dogs. I enjoy teaching and playing with my dogs. I receive more positive feedback from my dogs, and from people who see them, than from any other thing I've ever done. I derive pleasure from my animals. Remember that the fault is yours when Duchess doesn't do what she has been told. Be calm and closely examine how you confused her. Your dog loves you and wants to please you. Be patient.

Rule 5: Think Like a Dog

Human beings have been gifted with a complex brain and the ability to reason. In 1828, when Noah Webster compiled his famous dictionary, he collected 70,000 words in the English language. Most children understand hundreds of words by the age of two. Dogs, on the other hand, have smaller and less complex brains. They lack the logic and reasoning that allow humans to master information quickly. The number of words a bright dog understands is small. However, your dog can learn many words that will close the communication gap. Duchess's progress is limited only to your ability and time. Teaching her the twenty-word language you will learn in this book is like programming a small computer in her brain. Later, when you command her by using a word or set of words, her response will follow automatically.

To accomplish this, it is necessary that you think like a

dog. Duchess can't think on your level. You possess the reasoning and superior intelligence to bridge the gap. Identify her confusion. It may be caused by hearing a word that rhymes with another word or seeing a hand signal that is poorly fed into her "computer." There might be distractions that affect your dog's performance. Distractions such as sounds, scents, people, and other animals can make it hard for Duchess to concentrate on you and your command. If you think like a dog and talk to her on her own level, you'll be a happy dog owner!

Rule 6: Respect Your Dog as a "Person"

Treat your puppy as you would treat another person you might meet. When you walk through your front door and greet the family, give a short burst of attention to Duchess, too. If you find her too excited when she sees you, make her sit and give her a scratch on the head. Then be sure to release her from the *sit* command. Always be happy to see your dog when a separation has occurred and let her know it. It's not only polite, but you'll find your dog will love you even more.

Rule 7: Praise Rather Than Punish

Stress the positive, lightly touch on the negative, and turn that negative into a positive. It's simple! Encourage the things you want your puppy to do and discourage the *bad* habits.

The idea of turning a negative into a positive is essential. Like humans, puppies that are complimented for a job well done, rather than condemned for a few mistakes along the way, will progress faster and be happier. For example, some puppies instinctively take mouthfuls of food and travel with them a short distance away from the food bowl. Then they drop the food and leave it while they return to the large bowl of food. Suppose you see Duchess doing this. Scold her with the word *bad,* and immediately take her over to the food that fell on the floor. Encourage her to eat the dropped food and praise her as she wipes the floor clean with her tongue. Go to the next deposit of food and continue the process until the floor is free of dog food. Continue praising your puppy throughout the process and allow her to return to the main bowl. The next night monitor her eating and require that she clean up the dog food she drops before returning to her bowl. If you've had this problem for some time, a week of monitoring might be needed. In this example, you told your puppy that a certain behavior was bad, and you praised her when she corrected it. In correcting her eating habits, you guided her into being such a good puppy that it would've made her mother cry with pride!

There are several good ways of praising and encouraging your puppy for correct behavior. Small pieces of meat or cheese make an excellent incentive. A good chew toy at the end of a training session is another. An intermixing of play and work is fun for both. My favorite two rewards are a good scratch and using the word *good*. Puppies not only love to be scratched, but each one has a favorite place to be scratched. Note the back paw tap dance when you find that certain spot! The word *good* is a super reward. Use it constantly. In general, know what pleases your puppy, and try to vary the rewards. Praise and encourage her often.

Throughout the book, I will be suggesting the use of food treats for all new training. I support the use of food as a motivator for all initial training because nothing works better. Using food rewards make new lessons quicker to learn and more fun for the puppy. However, once the new behavior is learned, phase out the food and substitute other rewards like petting and the word *good*. It is important that your puppy listen to you whether you have food or not. Use food treats for new training and only intermittently with previously learned lessons.

Punishment per se should never be used. This term implies rough treatment. Never hit your puppy. You want your puppy to love you, not to fear you. If you are presently hitting your puppy as a punishment, stop and try using a squirt of water from a squirt bottle instead. The squirt bottle will enable you to correct your puppy quickly and from a distance. Rather than punish your puppy, try to discipline her. A disciplined dog is one that has developed self-control and obedience. Disciplining your puppy will be treated in more detail later. The basic principle is not to let your puppy get away with anything you consider undesirable. The discipline should be gauged to the severity of the crime. In all cases, Duchess should understand that she did something wrong and that she was bad. If a large mess is involved, a long *sit-stay* is in order, so that she can watch while you clean up the mess. As your puppy watches you, tell her she's been *bad*. Restricting her to a certain area is sometimes an effective method of disciplining her when you are angry or upset. Some area that is away from the family but still within your view is best. The puppy must be left there and corrected if she starts to leave the spot. It's your responsibility to release her from the area, not her choice. In this process, there is a delay in turning the negative into a positive. In this case, it would be a good idea to give a quick training session to put your puppy in good standing. You'll find your puppy awfully glad to be back in your good graces.

Most people do not discipline their dogs when friends are visiting. Thus, when the Smiths come over, Duchess runs wild and knows that company means recess! She has been taught that anything goes in front of guests. If you make humane corrections, your friends won't mind. Friends and strangers will understand your corrections and appreciate them. You and your puppy will gain their respect. There is a chance they'll even be looking forward to their next visit to your home.

Rule 8: Praise or Correct Immediately

The quicker you are to praise or correct, the better off you will be. When Duchess does something that deserves a reaction on your part, give her the proper feedback

19

instantly. Young children who have had a good time drawing with crayons on the kitchen wall will make the connection between their punishment and the crime, even when they are caught and punished hours later. But puppies are different. It's not highly effective to discipline a puppy for something unless you catch her in the act and discipline her immediately, so that she associates the discipline with the misconduct. Praise works the same way. It must be immediate, so that Duchess can associate the praise with the good thing that she does. Late praise can be misinterpreted by the puppy for some misdeed or just happily accepted without understanding why. In canine feedback, the quicker the praise or discipline is applied, the better the puppy will learn.

Rule 9: Ask Only the Possible

If you ask Duchess to fetch the mailman, you are allowing your puppy to fail because the mailman is too heavy and most likely, he's very unwilling. Likewise, if your puppy won't hold anything in her mouth, you shouldn't ask her to retrieve. Stress the positive and allow your puppy only to succeed. The complicated tricks you see canine stars do on TV are accomplished through a gradual training process. The dogs are taught several things, each progressing in difficulty, until they master the final trick. If, for some reason, you slip and ask your puppy to do something beyond her ability, either allow her to do a portion of what you have asked or physically aid her in succeeding. A shower of praise should then follow. With experience you'll avoid the commands that get you into trouble.

Rule 10: Give a Command Only Once

Why should Duchess react quickly to your command if she knows you'll repeat it again and again? She won't. Your puppy soon learns that she doesn't have to react until your second, third, or fourth command. In Chapter 10 you will be introduced to the word *hurry*. This word will get your puppy to obey the original command faster and provide you with an alternative to repeating it. Hurry tells Duchess that you know she has heard you the first time and that she should get moving. You'll see your **puppy** perform the command that was given to her seconds earlier without having to repeat the original command.

Rule 11: Release Each Command

When you command Duchess into a position such as *down or sit,* make her stay in that position until you release her. If you don't, your **puppy** should theoretically stay there for life. The **puppy** whose owner doesn't follow this rule will shortly break from that position when her master's back is turned. The **puppy** knows from experience that she won't be corrected. In this case, the master is reinforcing the **puppy**'s disobedience.

Another example is when you're heading out on the town, and Duchess wants to come with you so badly that she's pushing people out of the way to get to the front door. You call her away from the door, tell her to *stay,* and then leave without her. Not seeing you, she decides to move, and is never corrected for breaking a *stay.* Again, you are at fault.

When you give a positioning command, you are committed to enforcing the command and later releasing your **puppy**. Get her used to this. Don't allow her to make the decision. In Chapter 10, I will introduce you to the release word *okay* and how to use it.

Rule 12: Allow Your Dog to Be Good

Leaving Duchess alone in the house with an overflowing trash can might be asking for trouble - - especially if you have the remnants of last night's chicken dinner in it. If Duchess has a good time with the trash once, she might just make it a weekly adventure. This negligence on your part applies to many things that make you upset with your **puppy**. A sandwich left on the coffee table when you leave to answer the door might not be there when you return. Your **puppy** has received a sufficient and tasty reward and is likely to try it again in the future.

21

Remove all temptations that might cause Duchess to be bad. If she likes chewing on a special throw rug, remove it while you are out of the room. When you are in the room together, replace it and be ready to correct her if she nears it. Place china or other breakable items out of the reach of your **puppy's** tail. When you leave food near the edge of your kitchen countertop, you are tempting your **puppy** needlessly.

The only time you want to present temptations to Duchess is when you are there to make the correction. Let's take the earlier example of your leaving your **puppy** in the same room with the sandwich on the coffee table. The next time you are in approximately the same circumstance, leave the room and wait quietly. Duchess will probably get up and check out what you were eating. She might be coming only to sniff it, but when she does, race into the room and scold her for her attempt to eat your sandwich. If she hasn't budged toward the delicacy she has been smelling, praise her when you enter the room. You might even offer her a small piece of it as a reward.

Rule 13: Train Before Dinner

Practice makes perfect. Unfortunately, time is always in short supply. This rule requires that you run Duchess through a series of commands before you release her to eat dinner. It can be a fifteen-second or a five-minute drill. But be consistent, and make sure you do it before each meal. When dinner is a reward, you'll find that your **puppy** will listen and try hard.

Review the commands that should be familiar to your **puppy**. Do not cover new material at this time. New material can be introduced when you have some spare time. These short sessions will strengthen existing skills. You will both progress quickly, and your **puppy** will enjoy working for her meals. Even with dinner as a final reward, make sure that you verbally reward your **puppy** for doing well. Additional training can be given after your **puppy** has had a chance to eat a bit. This second session, ending in her final release to go eat, is also effective.

Rule 14: Play After Other Training Sessions

Except for dinner training, all training sessions should end with play. Either put Duchess on a *stay* and find her favorite toy or, if possible, have her find it. You're playing with her will be a great reward for her efforts, and it will also give her something to look forward to during every training session. The excitement will show. Experiment with the toys you use. The favorite in my house is a sock for pulling.

Rule 15: Record Your Dog's Progress

Though the Twenty Magic Words are simple, it is still necessary to record your progress on paper. Your **puppy**'s progress requires you to be organized. It is the only way consistency and progress can be achieved. If there are other people in your household, this list should be posted, and everyone should be informed of additions and their meaning. Having your **puppy**'s language written down on paper will allow you to examine it periodically to note her strengths and weaknesses. With this information you'll be able to overcome her weaknesses and note where additional words might be added.

Many people believe that having an obedient puppy is a luxury beyond their reach. They don't realize that they can train their puppy to obey them. I am often asked by people if I can train their dog, or they tell me that they've always wanted to send their dog off to obedience school. For a dog to listen to its owner, the owner must participate in the dog's training. Behind every obedient dog is an owner who cares and loves his or her dog. Be very conscious of the rules and your violations of them. Soon you'll condition yourself, and the rules will be a way of life for you. You'll be proud and happy that you understand your puppy and that he understands you.

#5 Your Dog's First Word

As a starting point for all communication with Fifi, it is essential that she recognize her name. It is the first and most important word in her vocabulary. People have names, places have names, and objects have names.

Puppies initially learn their names quickly and with ease. If you are getting a puppy, I caution you to carefully select a name you like. Often owners will select lengthy names that later need to be shortened to a nickname. Imagine turning to your puppy and commanding, "Sir Edward Dungsburg of Lake Burrough, *come*!" Both you and your puppy will be old before he understands and follows the command.

The purpose of this chapter is to teach you how you can reinforce Fifi's reaction to her name. You must remember that any puppy living with people hears thousands of words in a day. Unless you take special care, she can't possibly filter out just those that pertain to her. You can help by using her name first whenever you speak to her. It is especially important to use her name first to get her attention before giving her a command.

A drill to practice or just to evaluate Fifi's attention to her name can be done easily. While Fifi is sitting or lying down, begin to walk around the room. Start by holding a food reward, preferably small pieces. Fifi, knowing that you have food, will be all eyes. Continue the circling until her attention fades. When it does, call her name. As soon as her attention focuses on you, throw her a treat. Repeat this several times. If Fifi reacts quickly to her name or watches constantly, you've passed with flying colors! You might want to try the drill again just after you've fed Fifi. This will eliminate food as her main incentive for watching you and will allow her to react mainly to her name. If your **puppy** lacks the desire to watch you or responds slowly at hearing her name, practice this drill daily for a while.

Although using your **puppy's** name to begin a command seems easy and logical, many break this rule. Some **puppy** owners forget to use their **puppy's** name when they give a command. Others give the command first, followed by the **puppy's** name. In the example, "Come on, Fifi," the owner will get Fifi's attention after the command is given, not giving the **puppy** a fair chance to follow the command.

An additional, but avoidable, complication stems from the fact that many owners will also refer to their **puppy** as Baby, Honey, Sugar, Sweetie, Puppy, or Cutie. Boy and Girl are other variants that are sometimes used alone and sometimes used in conjunction with another name as in "Come on, Fifi-girl!" These all are nice descriptive nicknames, but the name needed to get your **puppy's** attention immediately is her own! I suggest you avoid variants and use pet names on your deserving spouse or friend to make your **puppy's** life easier.

As you can see, using your puppy's name as the start of all communication is important. You'll be getting her attention and then communicating your wishes to her in a logical sequence. The feedback words in Chapter 6 and some of the special commands in Chapter 10 will be your only exceptions.

#6 Feedback Words: Good, Bad, and No

In Chapter 4, Rules 7 and 8, the importance of feedback as a means of communicating to your puppy what is preferred and what is unacceptable was discussed. Your puppy will quickly learn what these feedback words mean. The words in this chapter, along with the words *hurry* and *okay,* found in Chapter 10, are your most useful tools of guidance. These words needn't follow your puppy's name. They can be used separately because they receive the full and immediate attention of your puppy.

The Word Good

An owner who is happy with his or her puppy may use a variety of words: "That's my girl!" "Okay!" "All right!" "You're a fine animal!" Generally, the meaning gets communicated to Skipper through the owner's body position and tone of voice. You must restrict your praise to the word *good.* Being consistent in your words of praise will ensure that Skipper will understand that what he did was good. Leave nothing to chance! You want Skipper to understand how happy he has made you in being a good puppy. Remember, encourage in Skipper only the behavior that you want. Give him the feedback quickly and say the word *good* in an excited tone.

The Words Bad and No

Bad and *no* are the only negative words you need to use. Both words are needed to correct negative behavior: the first for an act already committed, the second for one about to be committed or in progress. There will be times when, like the rest of us, you will want to hurl curse words or milder invectives at your puppy. If you do, you will be defeating your purpose. Try your best to limit yourself to *bad* and *no.* When used correctly and consistently, they are the words that will best communicate your views.

Use the word *bad* when Skipper has committed a serious violation and needs to be given a very stern reprimand. If he growls at your neighbor's child, use his collar to control him and make him sit. Then scold him, using the word *bad.* Often your puppy will need to be disciplined for making a mess. Here a time factor is involved while you are cleaning up the mess. Skipper should *sit* and watch you work. As you clean up, tell him how *bad* he's been. Occasionally, if your puppy lacks the motivation necessary in a training session, it is helpful to call him *bad.* The shock of it can often get your puppy to try a little harder. When he does, praise the heck out of him, and he will maintain his enthusiasm. In general, the word *bad* will set back your puppy's ears, put his tail down, and his face will take on a sad and ashamed expression.

The word *no* will evoke a quite different reaction from Skipper. In this case, he will fear a correction and act very submissively. Use this word when you want to give a quick warning about some temptation that could lead him to being bad. If your puppy ignores the warning, a subsequent correction is required. If he is sniffing some freshly baked cookies near the edge of the kitchen counter, a strong *"No!"* is in order. When he turns away from the sniffing, praise him for listening to you. If your puppy runs toward a busy street, you can easily thwart him with the command, *"No!* Skipper, *come."* Here his direction toward the traffic is suddenly stopped, and he is called back to safety. The word *no* can also be used in conjunction with other words to communicate to your **puppy** what action should not occur. This can be an advanced warning or a means of scolding in an explanatory way. Later the phrases *no bark, no eat, no sniff,* or *no beg* might be incorporated into your **puppy**'s language. I have found their application and the application of other combinations extremely valuable.

In summing up, the word *bad* is used when it's too late to say *"No!"* Don't worry about which word you use. Both are extremely negative responses to your puppy's unacceptable behavior, and the message will be understood. Use the one that fits the situation or use them both. What's important is that you be consistent in using only these two words, giving the feedback as quickly as possible, and coordinating your tone of voice to match the word's message.

#7 Major Directives: Stay, Go, and Come

The directives *stay*, *go*, and *come* request no movement, a movement away from the speaker, or a movement toward the speaker. They are key words that are used by themselves or in combination with other words. I call them major directives because these three words will enable you to direct Rover anywhere. The need for lateral movement in your puppy is not that important, because the *go* command is completely directional with the aid of a hand signal. You merely call Rover to you and send him where you wish. The list of uses of these words is long and practical. Each word and its uses will be discussed in this chapter. Rover's understanding of each word will depend on his ability, your ability to follow the rules in Chapter 4, and how well you follow the training methods described for each word. *Stay, go,* and *come* are the three most important commands to teach your puppy and are among the easiest for him to learn.

The Word Stay

The *stay* command is given when you want Rover to remain in the place or position you've specified. It could be on the front porch or in a *sit* position while you make his dinner. The *stay* command is a must. It's the basic command in disciplining your puppy. You can't discipline him if he's bounding around the room enjoying himself! In training your puppy, the *stay* command is necessary for his control and attention. A dog that can do a good *stay* can be taken anywhere, because he can be controlled. If Rover likes to gnaw on smaller helpless dogs, a *stay* will keep him from making chew toys out of the poor little things. If the shoe is on the other paw and you own that small helpless puppy, a *stay* will allow you to protect it. If Rover is retrieving a ball on the other side of the street and is about to return with it just as a car is approaching, the *stay* could save his neck, tail, hair, and other important parts. Teaching your **puppy** the *stay* command will help his behavior and keep him safe.

Start the training with Rover in a comfortable position and on leash to aid your control. Use the puppy's name first, followed by the word *stay*. Walk away from him but keep a close eye on him. If he breaks forward, quickly push him backward to the original position. Repeat the command, "Rover, *stay*!" and try again. The *stay* command should not be repeated if Rover is staying adequately (see Chapter 4, Rule 10). Use the word *good,* but expect Rover to break the *stay* command initially, and be there for the correction. He will learn quickly that the *good is* given to praise him and that it's not a release command. The release command is the word *okay.* It will be discussed in Chapter 10. After a short period of practicing the command, return to your puppy and release him. Initially it's a good idea to train Rover that you always return to him before you release him. This will help him to learn faster.

After a week of practicing the *stay* command, Rover should understand it easily. It is now time for you to make a pro of him. Practice the *stay* command in different situations that might cause him to break the command. Be sure that you correct him quickly and reinforce the *stay* in his mind. Below are a few variations you might try in practicing the *stay* command:

1. Give the command when your puppy is sitting, lying down, or standing.

2. Increase the time of the *stay*.

3. Drop a book or clang some potlids to distract your puppy.

4. Go outside and try increasing your distance from your puppy.

5. Try public places but remember to think of your puppy's safety in the event it breaks.

6. Leave the room, but watch secretly.

7. Add distractions by having neighbors and their dogs walk in front of Rover.

Once you've achieved the standard of excellence you have set for the *stay* command, be consistent and don't allow Rover to deviate from it. He will occasionally test you to find out if you'll make a correction. He should understand that once put on a stay, any crawling is wrong. This inching, if not corrected immediately, will be considered progress by him, and he will think that it's okay.

The only exception I make for my dogs on *stay* is while they wait for me. Let's say that I'm visiting a friend's house who doesn't own a dog. Out of courtesy to him and his home's lack of dog hair, I *down* my dogs on his front porch and tell them to *stay*. In this case, I allow them to readjust and make themselves comfortable. They will move to the soft welcome mat or maybe to the corner of the porch to get a better view. If they stay on the porch, they understand they are fine, and I won't make a correction. Dogs view things by territories and are easily taught, without a barricade, to stay within certain boundaries. It could be

31

a doorway, an open garage, or even a sidewalk. If you practice the *stay* command occasionally, your **puppy** will continue to take the command seriously.

The Word Go

The *go* command is given whenever you desire Rover to move away from you. The uses are practical and helpful. You can direct him to a person, place, or thing. Whenever you need to deliver virtually anything to someone - - a message, a can of pop, the newspaper, or even a dirty shirt - - allow your **puppy** to do it. If Rover is in danger of being made into home plate because your softball team decides they want to drink at your house, direct him under the table or upstairs until the danger subsides.

Sending Rover with the *go* command to retrieve an article can save you much effort, and it's cheaper than hiring a butler! It might be a piece of paper in the yard, your slippers in the closet, or even his own brush for grooming. The *go* command can also be used as a warning when Rover gets in the way. If you're carrying

the groceries in and Rover is lying in your path, tell him to *go* and then praise him for obliging. You might even let him help you carry in the groceries. On your next trip from the car, hand him the box of crackers. He'll enjoy helping you.

The word *go* is sometimes used for correction. When Rover is at the dinner table begging for some scraps or maybe a plate of his own, tell him, "*No!*" and tell him, "*Go!*" Teaching your **puppy** the *go* command will

32

allow you to direct him anywhere for whatever reason you desire.

Start training for the word *go* by having your **puppy** sit and dropping a piece of food 5 feet (1.5 m) in front of him. Position yourself next to him in the heel position and say, "Rover, *go!*" as you direct him with your left hand. Run with him up to the meat and praise him for finding and eating it. Your *go* hand signal should resemble the one pictured. Be careful to direct him accurately. As Rover learns that it's easy food, increase the distance of the reward, and hold your position unless he needs some help. Soon you should be able to hide the food behind obstacles, and your friend will find it quickly. This method can be used to direct Rover to a person by having the person hold the reward and, upon Rover's arrival, present it to him.

The Word Come

The last of the major directives is the word *come*. Upon hearing this word, Rover should immediately come toward you. Once he arrives, he should sit in front of you and give you his full attention. This command is useful whenever you want to call him to do anything, or even when you might just be lonely. The *come* command can also be used in conjunction with other commands. In the example, "Rover, *come get* it!" the *come* is used to guide Rover toward you so that he can find what you want him to get. Whenever the action you want him to perform is between you and him, use the *come* command. Learn by watching his reaction. If the object is too far away on either side of the come path back to you, you have three choices. Move in a more direct line with Rover's assignment, use a hand signal to direct him to the proper side, or call him to you and redirect him to the desired spot using the command *go.* The word *come* is by far the most important command for him to know. Only a small percentage of the dog population executes it dependably. With a little correct training, your **puppy** will quickly respond every time.

To prepare training for the word *come,* get a clothesline-sized rope approximately 25 feet (7.6 m) and attach a snap or dog harness clip to one end. Both can be purchased at any hardware store. A special training collar is also extremely helpful. This collar is sometimes referred to as a choke chain because it acts as a slip knot would. When one of the two end loops is pulled, the collar tightens around the puppy's neck. The name associated with these collars infers strangling and suffocation. Though they can be misused and though some collars on the market do inflict discomfort, most are not cruel if used properly. I find the name "choke chain" upsetting. I ask all dog owners to refer to them as training collars instead. A training collar will give you that extra amount of control needed for corrections. The training collar has resulted in some accidental deaths, when dogs jumped over a fence or bush and got their collars caught in the process. Religiously remove the collar after each training session. To purchase one, measure the distance around your puppy's neck and shop for a collar that is approximately 2 inches (5 cm) longer. As you place the training collar over the puppy's head, form the letter "P" as you are looking toward your puppy. This allows the collar to release easily after a correction when your puppy is in a heel position.

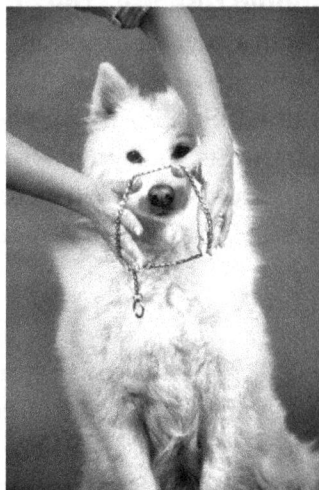

Start the training by making Rover *sit* and telling him to *stay.* Then attach the rope to his collar by using the snap. Go 10 feet (3 m) from him and stand facing him. Hold the rope in both hands and have it almost taut. Have a piece of food ready to reward him. Correct him for any violations of the *stay.* Try a short pause to get his attention and to prepare him to react to your wishes. Call your puppy by using his name and the word *come*. If he doesn't move toward you instantly, gently pull on the rope to get him moving and praise him. As the puppy is coming toward you, pull up the slack in the rope and back up in a straight line. Taking up the slack will allow you to control his *sit* upon arrival. Backing is used initially for motivating your puppy to catch up to you as if he were chasing you in play. Guide him into a *sit* position in front of you and hand him the reward. Be sure to praise him throughout this whole process. Try this several times, and then play with him as a reward. In your next session, review your puppy's accomplishments and increase the distance of the *come*. When your puppy has the command down pat, remove the rope and try it. If he fails to come immediately when called, run up to him and snap on the lead. Work with the rope a few more times and then try it again without it. Remember patience and praise are your best tools.

Whenever you find your puppy responding slowly to the *come* command, a quick practice session will reinforce it in his mind. I keep doggie cookies around the house in different areas to reward my dogs occasionally. If you want to call your puppy and have a food reward available, use it. I assure you, Rover will come faster the next time. Spoil your puppy. He deserves it!

If you have a large house or yard where your puppy might be out of calling range, a bell or whistle can help. Decide on the signal: try your own whistling skills or buy a whistle or a bell. I give a distinctive two-part whistle in a special tone. Since my orthodontist painfully straightened my incisors, my whistle is always handy. To teach your puppy to respond to a whistle or a bell, go back to the rope training but replace the vocal command with the whistle or bell. Follow the same steps as before. With a little work, your puppy will come to you when you use either.

The three major directives - - *stay, go,* and *come* - - will enable you to direct your puppy anywhere with ease and leave him there, if that is your wish. Your puppy will be happy because he finally understands you, spends more time with you, gets recognition when he pleases you, and relishes the training sessions because of the special treats you use as rewards. Your puppy is now in your control. You now have the means to ensure his safety when you show him off in public.

The First Seven Magic Words

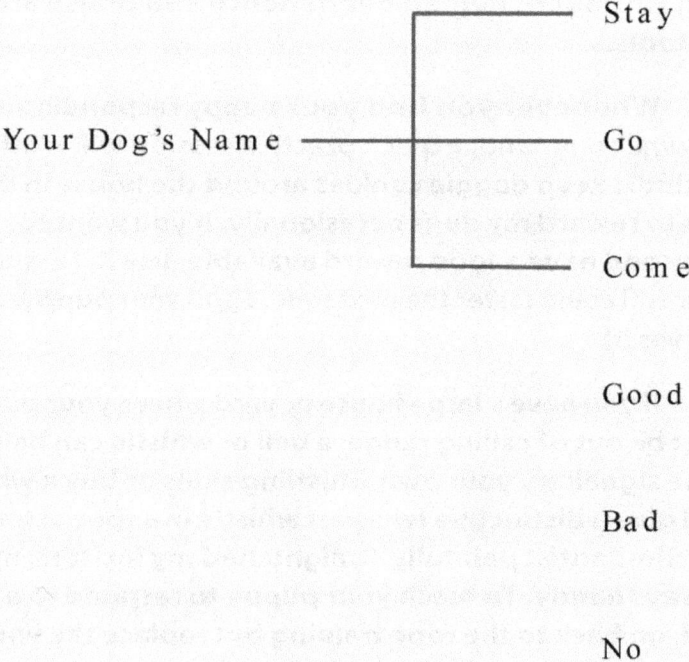

Stay

Your Dog's Name ──────── Go

Come

Good

Bad

No

#8 Body Positions:
Sit and Down

In the previous chapters you learned how to get your puppy's attention, how to communicate approval or disapproval, and how to direct or leave your puppy anywhere. This chapter concerns itself with Tinker's body positions.

The three major positions a dog assumes are sitting, lying down, and standing. In this chapter I will introduce only the *sit* and the *down* commands and their respective training. To keep Tinker's language simple and practical, the *stand* command will not be covered at this time. Chapter 12 will cover it and many other useful words that can be added after you have laid the foundation.

The *sit* and the *down* commands are often used by owners in a confusing manner. Often, they are given by using more words than are necessary and using the same words in different commands. Some examples of these are: "Sit up!" "Sit down!" "Lay down!" and "Lie down!" I remind you of this poor communication and ask that you be incredibly careful to correct any bad habits you've formed.

The *sit* is a position dogs use to enable them to rest their haunches while supporting themselves with their front legs. This command can be used for discipline, instruction, safety, courtesy, and to gain your puppy's attention. Once the *sit* command is given, the puppy should remain in the *sit* position forever, theoretically, until he is released by you. The release word *okay* will be introduced in Chapter 10. Notice that even though you haven't used the word *stay,* the puppy shouldn't budge, just as if you had used it. For this reason, when a longer

37

sit is necessary, use the command "Tinker, *sit. Stay*!" Using the *stay* command will reinforce the idea that he shouldn't budge. The *sit*, though a semi resting position, can be a very boring command for a **puppy** left in that position **too long**, and a bored **puppy** is tired, unhappy, and unacceptable. The **puppy** put on a long *sit* will start to shift its front paws as they tire. This could lead to the **puppy**'s breaking the *stay*. Once again, it's your fault. If not corrected for this, the **puppy** may develop the bad habit of shifting its weight, even while doing short *sits*. When practicing a long *sit-stay*, use your head and watch Tinker's expression to gauge the length of the *stay*. A three-minute *stay* is usually plenty for a **puppy**.

The *down* is a position in which Tinker's body is on the floor with his rear legs under him and his front legs extended. The *down* command is useful in long *stays because* the **puppy** is more comfortable. The uses and training associated with the *sit* also apply to the *down* command. Like the *sit*, once the *down* command is given, the **puppy** should remain in the *down* until released. Add the word *stay* when longer periods are desired. When you call Tinker and *down* him at your feet, be careful that you release him before he breaks the applied *stay*.

Train your **puppy** for the *sit* and the *down* commands at the same time. This is convenient, since with both commands you must release your **puppy** so that you can repeat them. Find an area for training that is free from distractions and grab some treats for your **puppy**. Call Tinker and give him a small reward for coming. Your **puppy** already uses the positions. All you must do is teach him to assume the *sit* or the *down* position when you give the command.

Start by saying, "Tinker, *sit*!" If your **puppy** doesn't move

38

immediately to a *sit* position, guide him gently but quickly into one. Then reward and praise him. The training collar can be used to help you guide him; pull up on the collar while pushing down on his less attractive end. The *stay* command should be added initially to reinforce the fact that your **puppy** should remain in that position. Now try the command, "Tinker, *down!*" If necessary, guide him quickly into the *down* position. Then reward and praise him. Continue alternating the commands. You should find that Tinker will progress rapidly. Don't allow the training to get boring. Move on to other training or have a play session with your **puppy**. The next day you will find that your **puppy** will be ready to impress you again.

Continue the exercise daily until Tinker responds quickly to each command. As he quickens his response, be more conscious of his position. Some **puppies** will sit sloppily on the side of their hip or even put a paw out to the side. Determine the standard that you want and be consistent in correcting Tinker for any violations immediately. Approach him and physically adjust his position to what you want. Do not reward or praise him until he has achieved the position you demand of him each time. Occasionally Tinker will have a temporary "lapse of memory," and will do nothing upon hearing a command. He is merely testing you. You should move quickly to make a correction. Do not repeat commands! If Tinker becomes accustomed to your repeating a command, he will soon wait until you have repeated it the second or third time before responding. Make corrections for any forward movement by pushing your **puppy** back to the original spot.

Now that Tinker has mastered the *sit* and the *down* commands, increase your distance from him and practice. No matter how good your puppy is, you'll find that there is a certain distance beyond which you'll lose control. Find the greatest distance where you still have control, and slowly increase your range over many sessions. Remember, always allow your puppy to succeed! You will progress with him much more quickly.

You now have taught your puppy his name and eight basic commands. *Good, bad,* and *no* taught the puppy right from wrong. *Stay, go,* and *come* directed him to remain where he is, leave you, or come to you. *Sit* and *down* enabled your puppy to assume a certain position. You also learned that you could use combinations of commands, such as *sit-stay* and *down-stay,* to get your puppy to remain in a position until released. If your puppy has mastered these commands, you are now ready to teach the secondary commands.

The First Nine Magic Words

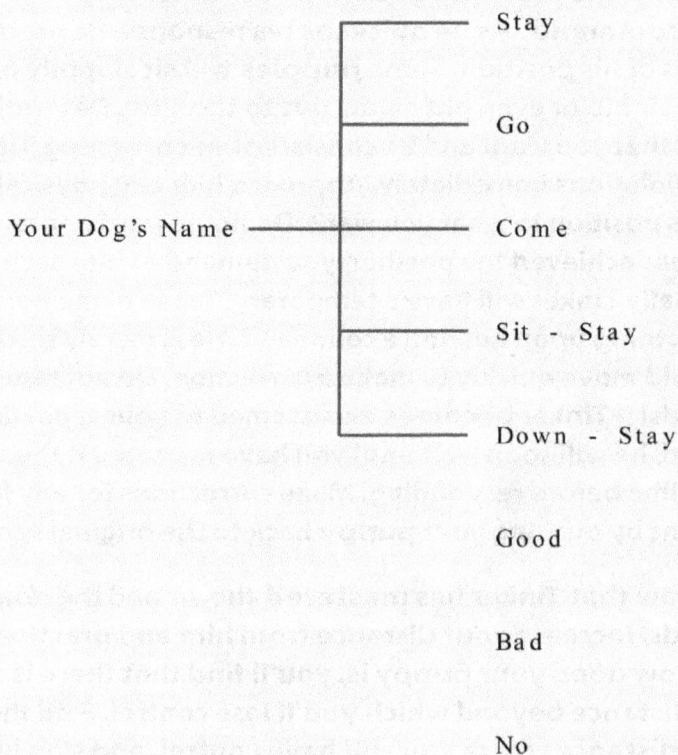

```
                                    ┌──────── Stay

                                    ├──────── Go

        Your Dog's Name ────────────┼──────── Come

                                    ├──────── Sit - Stay

                                    └──────── Down - Stay


                                             Good


                                             Bad


                                             No
```

#9 Secondary Commands: Hold, Get, Drop, Bring, Up, and Nose

Secondary commands are used in combination with the major directives *go* and *come* and the body position words *sit* and *down.* These commands can also be used separately when preceded by your puppy's name. By teaching Brandy these secondary commands, you will enlarge your range of control over her. You will be able to ask her for the specific action you desire. Because of the special training you will give her, she will be able to respond effortlessly.

When a secondary command is used correctly in conjunction with a major directive, the sentence conveys the message to your puppy without any confusion. An example of this is, "Brandy, *go, get* it." Here the puppy's attention is obtained on the first word. The second word starts Brandy moving away from you, and the third word directs her to look for the article and grab it.

The idea that a puppy can understand a string of commands in a sentence is a radical one in dog training. Most dog people say that it's impossible. I know that dogs can understand sentences and can prove it with my dogs. Your puppy or dog will try to please. If they can pick up the key words in their master's sentence, or maybe a helpful hand signal, they will easily obey the command.

As you and Brandy advance in this language, you'll understand why the logical sentence avoids the confusion and stress put on her previously. There will be no limits on the communication you can have with her. Two short sentences will enable Brandy to go to another room, find a specific article, return, and drop it at a previously mentioned spot.

A secondary command can be linked to a body position, as in the example, "Brandy, *sit* and *hold* it." Here you first obtain Brandy's attention. The word *sit* gets her to assume the position, and the *hold* commands her to grab the article you hand her. The key words *sit* and *hold* should be emphasized as the command is given. As soon as Brandy understands the *sit* and the *hold* commands separately, combining them in one sentence is quicker for you and easier for her. The command can be used whenever you want her help carrying anything. Even if you can manage a load, get her involved, and she'll be happy from her nose down to her wagging tail.

The secondary commands are also used when no major movement or specific body position is required. In the example, "Brandy, *drop* it," you are getting her attention and then commanding her to release the article. The *go* and *come* are not used, because Brandy is already in the correct area for the *drop.* Likewise, a specific body position isn't necessary to drop the article in a particular spot. Your goal is to command the desired action in a logical sequence, using a minimum of words to accomplish your purpose. Requesting a *sit* might help Brandy to aim more carefully when dropping your empty pop can in the trash. A missed *drop* could leave drops of pop on the kitchen floor, not to mention your being sentenced to Brandy's doghouse by your otherwise amiable housekeeper!

The words "it" and "and," though not counted in the Twenty Magic Words, are used frequently. I recommend these additives because they complete a command in a logical sentence structure without adding any confusion. Call it a small compromise for humans. The sentences can be delivered gracefully, and your **puppy** will still show ease in following your orders. The additive "and" serves to separate two-word commands for Brandy and makes it easier for her to understand the sentence command. The additive "it" completes the sentence.

42

Since the word "it" is not accentuated, it will not confuse her.

The Word Hold

The first four of the six secondary commands are the words *hold, get, drop,* and *bring.* Each of these words represents a specific action involved in basic retrieves. The *hold* command will be learned first because in the *get, drop,* and *bring* commands it is essential that Brandy accept an article and *hold* it in her mouth. She will learn this word when you use it in the following sentence commands:

1. Brandy, *hold* it.

2. Brandy, *come, hold* it.

3. Brandy, *sit* and *hold* it.

4. Brandy, *down* and *hold* it.

In the first sentence Brandy is already close enough for you to hand her the article. When the *come* is inserted, you are requesting that Brandy make a debut and accept the item you wish her to *hold.* The sentences "Brandy, *sit* and *hold* it" and "Brandy, *down* and *hold* it" are useful in handing her an article and in reinforcing the command in Brandy's mind. A specific body position is helpful for her control and attention. Brandy should wait patiently until you give her a further command. This can be useful when there is an unexpected delay. For example, let's say your doorbell rings when Brandy is helping you carry something. Go to the door with her and say, "Brandy, *sit* and *hold* it." A stranger at the door gives your puppy a very tempting reason to *drop* the item, break the *stay,* and sniff the stranger. Watch in case you need to make a correction. Regardless of whether a correction is made, when the stranger leaves, remove the item from Brandy's mouth and praise her, play with her, and thoroughly enjoy her. If the time is short, tell her that she's *good.*

To teach Brandy to hold an object, first find an object

she enjoys holding. I'd suggest her favorite toy, since she undoubtedly has held it many times and has fond memories associated with it. Procure some tasty treats to reward her and call her to you. Ask her to *sit* , give the command, "Brandy, *hold* it," and place the article gently in her mouth. Remove the article immediately and reward her. If Brandy is extremely hesitant about holding her toy, try rubbing some of the reward on it. If she won't open her jaws, trick her with a piece of food. Begin to give her a piece of food, but when she opens her mouth, quickly place the article in it. Pull the article out, and then reward her with the food. If your **puppy** accepts the article but seems a bit startled, it's a good sign. You'd be startled too if your friend asked you to hold something in your mouth! Try offering the article again, and make sure that your **puppy** is rewarded quickly each time. You must use your judgment on how hard and long you work in the first training session. If your **puppy** accepts the object easily, continue. But remember that it's your obligation to keep the entire training session on a positive note. Be patient. Continue the training at your **puppy**'s pace for a few weeks if necessary.

The next step is to offer Brandy the article, position your free hand underneath her jaw to support it, and release your grip on the article. Do not press her upper and lower jaws together. This is uncomfortable for her and unnecessary. As soon as you are in the correct position, use your free hand to remove the article from her mouth and reward her. Repeat this many times until there is no need for your hand under her jaw. Brandy may test you to see if you will let her get by if she drops the article. If she makes the attempt, make the correction. If she starts to spit it out, put your hand under her jaw and repeat the command, "Brandy, *hold* it." If you are slow and the article falls to the floor, quickly place the article back in her mouth and command her to *hold* it.

Even though the remaining three sentences containing the *hold* command are easy, each should be practiced separately. The first command is, "Brandy, *come hold* it." **Place** her on a *stay* and walk 10 feet (3 m) away from **her. Turn** to her, hold out the article, and give her the command. **Help** her all you can at the beginning and remember to reward **her** when you remove the article from her mouth. The next two sentences, "Brandy, *sit* and *hold* it" and "Brandy, *down* and *hold* it," are also easy. Put your **puppy** in a standing position, say the commands, and **hand** her the article. If she doesn't assume the proper body position, help her into **it**, and offer her the article to hold. I say help because a severe correction will lessen her desire to **learn** the new material. Keep the duration of the *hold* short at first and reward **her.** You should also **train your puppy** to be able to hold an **item** while going from a *sit* to a *down* position and vice versa. In this case, repeating the *hold* part of the command reinforces the command and prevents any mistakes. Your **puppy** should continue to hold the article until you take it from her, **until** you give **her** the command to *drop* it, or until your **puppy's** great **recall** comes from heaven!

The training process for *hold is* easy because of the gradual steps. You've allowed Brandy to succeed in each step, and in the process the **learning has** been clear and quick. Continue by increasing the time an object is held and by using different objects. You'll find that Brandy hesitates to accept some articles because of their weight, size, shape, or composition. You'll also **find that in** the process of training she has picked up the hand signal for *hold.* Every time you told her to "*hold* it," she saw your hand coming toward her with an article for her to grab. You've conditioned **her not** only to your verbal command but to your **hand signal, thus making the** communication of the command easier for her to understand and obey.

The Word Get

You are now ready to teach the command *get.* In your **puppy's** new language, the *get* command will be restricted to the act of acquiring the article. **Some trainers insist that** *get* **means the** whole process of obtaining the article, holding it, bringing it, and either holding it or dropping it on arrival. In this case, *get* simply communicates the specific action desired.

The word *get* will increase your **puppy**'s vocabulary if you use it in the following sentences:

1. **Brandy,** *get* **it.**

2. **Brandy,** *go get* **it.**

3. **Brandy,** *come get* **it.**

4. **Brandy,** *go up* **and** *get* **It.**

Use the first of these when the article is within your **puppy**'s reach, and she doesn't need to move toward the article. In the second sentence, "Brandy, *go get* it," the *go* is inserted to send Brandy away from you and toward the article you've chosen for her to grab. When the *come* is inserted in the third sentence, you are requesting Brandy to travel toward you, find the article, and grab it. The last sentence, using the word *up,* will be discussed later in this chapter.

Dogs vary greatly in learning the word *get.* Many dogs instinctively chase an article that is thrown, and most of them will grab it. For the dog that does, teaching the *get* will involve only some additional control. The dog that presently isn't a good retriever has the instinct. It simply hasn't been developed. This fact makes it easy to teach your pet. Almost all dogs get daily practice in the *get* command in one way or another. They grab and carry toys around, and if a piece of food is thrown their way, they do a beautiful *get*! While the time it takes to teach different **puppies** the *get* command will vary, every **puppy** can learn it in a short time, and all of them will enjoy carrying out the command over and over.

The procedure for teaching Brandy to get an object

will use her favorite toy again and some tasty treats. It is essential that you get her in a playing mood. It will be more effective if you get down on the floor with her. Using her toy, play with her, and build up her interest in the toy. Drop the toy in front of her, and say in an enthusiastic voice, "Brandy, *get* it." Often tapping the floor next to the toy or wiggling the toy will help. If she succeeds in grabbing it, quickly take it away from her and reward her. If your puppy fails to grab it, go back to playing and try again. Use your own judgment as to when you should stop the lesson. Let your patience and your puppy's enthusiasm be your guide.

If Brandy doesn't seem to be catching on at all, the only answer is to get sneaky. Rub some of the tasty treat on the toy, play with it, and drop it again. This time when you drop it, leave a treat on top of it and give the command. Point out the treat if necessary. When Brandy reaches to grab it, place the toy, food, and all, in Brandy's mouth. Quickly remove the toy while praising her and allow her to chew the treat. Condition her by doing this over and over. Then repeat the steps but omit the treat. This time Brandy will move toward the toy to look for the food. When she gets close, help move the toy into her mouth. Praise her as you exchange the toy for a treat. Practice these initial steps until a high percentage of success is achieved. Soon your puppy will grab the toy quickly and receive her reward.

As you continue Brandy's training, throw the toy away from her while saying, "Brandy, *go, get* it." Her reactions will determine if additional steps are needed. It's essential that she run to the toy. If she does not, try the throw and the command again. This time run out with her. Put a leash on her for control if necessary. Then stop her at the right spot and reward her. If Brandy runs to the toy and then bounds off, put her on *stay,* and place the toy and a piece of food 10 feet (3 m) in front of her. Go back to Brandy and give her the command. This time when she stops for the food, be there with her, and keep her from continuing by using the leash. Once your puppy understands that she must travel immediately to the toy, use the techniques you've used earlier to help her pick it up.

When your puppy gets the toy with ease, try the command, "Brandy, *come, get* it." Place your puppy on *stay* and walk away from her. Turn toward her, place her toy 4 feet (1.2 m) in front of you, and give the command. In this exercise it is important that your puppy never be allowed to pass by the article she is asked to get. If she does, stop her immediately, push her back, and reinforce the *get* command. As you practice, move the toy closer to your puppy, but continue to keep it in a direct line between the two of you. You will find that your puppy adapts easily to this command because she understands the *come* and the *get* from her previous training.

To advance your **puppy** further on the *get,* try different articles and different locations in placing the articles. When you send your **puppy** to get an article, make sure that you avoid any confusion as to which article you're asking her to grab. Also, keep in mind that the *get* applies to her grabbing the article and not necessarily to her returning the article to you. Later the word *bring* will be utilized to get her to bring the article to you.

The Word Drop
The next secondary command for your **puppy** to learn is the *drop.* This refers to your **puppy**'s action of releasing an article she is holding. Using the major directives *stay, go,* and *come,* enables you to position your **puppy** anywhere. Once your **puppy** is positioned, the article can be dropped in a specific spot. The word *drop* will increase Brandy's vocabulary if you use it in the following sentences:

1. **Brandy,** *drop* **it.**

2. Brandy, *go drop* it.

3. Brandy, *come drop* it.

4. Brandy, *go up* and *drop* it.

The sentence "Brandy, *drop* it," can be used either when Brandy happens to be in a convenient spot for the article to be released or when the dropping is of major importance compared to the spot. If a particular spot is required, the major directives will be implemented. When the *drop* is used in conjunction with *go* and *come*, Brandy will delay the *drop* and travel in the specified direction looking for the proper *drop* zone and then drop it. I refer to it as a *drop* zone because there will be certain places that your puppy will understand are for dropping things. An empty box, the kitchen trash can, the toy box, the coffee table, and the clothes basket are just some of the places she'll quickly recognize. The more you practice, the more versatility you'll have in your *drop*. The last sentence, using the word *drop* and the word *up,* will be discussed later in this chapter.

To teach your puppy the word *drop,* find an article that would be uncomfortable for her to hold. The idea is to make your puppy want to *drop* it badly enough so that dropping it will be a reward for her. This article should not be the one you used in training your puppy for the *hold* command. Pick an object that she has a hard time holding. Since your puppy will be dropping it, make sure your selection can't be damaged and that you're on a carpeted floor. You might try a screwdriver, a tablespoon, a hair roller, an egg whisk, or even a set of metal measuring spoons.

With the proper article and some treats in hand, put Brandy in a *sit* and have her *hold* the article. Call in an excited tone, "Brandy, *drop* it!" At the same time, offer her a treat and gently knock the article out of her mouth, praising her as you do so. Repeat this exercise until Brandy starts dropping the article on her own to eat the food you're offering. If you still have trouble, wait a longer period on the *drop,* switch the article to make it less pleasing to hold, or offer her something she can't refuse for the treat. Your puppy should catch on quickly.

When using the *drop* command, it is unwise to catch the article as your puppy drops it. If you reach out to catch it, Brandy will soon begin to hold it until you reach out for it. It will become a hand signal for her to drop the article. This will be undesirable when you want her to *drop* something far away from you with a verbal command only. You won't be there to give her a hand signal. Also, if you send your puppy to deliver the article to someone, you'll want her to *hold* it until the article is taken from her mouth.

The procedure for teaching the command, "Brandy, *go drop* it," is an easy one. Ideally, it is best to have a large empty room that is free from all distractions and a large receptacle to catch the article dropped. Realistically, an empty box in an empty corner will do. The corner will direct her attention to the box you've placed in it and control her path of travel between you and the corner. To make a *drop* easy for your puppy, the box needs to be about four inches (10 cm) lower than your puppy's mouth when she is standing. If necessary, cut off the top few inches of the box. Use an article that is uncomfortable to hold. Have your puppy *sit* about one foot (30 cm) in front of the box and *hold* the article. Give the command, "Brandy, *go drop* it." If Brandy doesn't move, ease her into a standing position while you support the article beneath her jaw. Allow the article to drop when her mouth is over the box. Reward your puppy with a treat and a lot of praise. Repeat this until you're ready to increase the distance before the *drop,* change the placement of the box, or use a different type of *drop* zone.

The teaching of the sentence "Brandy, *come drop* it," is quite similar. Use the same article and box, but this time leave

Brandy in the corner in a *sit-stay* and have her *hold* the article. Place the box in front of her and position yourself in front of both. Say the command and, if necessary, help her to *drop* the article into the box. By this time, the *drop* and *come* are understood, and this exercise will be merely for practice.

The Word Bring

The secondary command *bring* directs Brandy to return immediately to the speaker while carrying the article she's holding or the one she's just picked up. Adding this word to the language is necessary because it represents a specific action not covered by the word *hold.* The command *bring* is a delivery to the person speaking. In Chapter 13, I will discuss the use of the word *take.* This word will allow Brandy to make a delivery of an article to another person. *Bring* is always used in a sentence having the following form: "Brandy, *come bring* it." Since your **puppy**'s action is always toward you, the major directive word *come* helps her understand you. You'll find that since the command is very descriptive, your **puppy** will easily learn it and perform it consistently.

To teach your **puppy** the *bring* command, put her in a *sit* position and have her *hold* her toy. Walk ten feet away from her, turn, and face her. Then give the command, "Brandy, *come bring* it." Praise her first attempt as she starts moving toward you. If she drops the article, run up to her, put the article in her mouth, and reinforce the *hold* command. Then quickly back up and repeat, "Brandy, *come bring* it." As your **puppy** comes up to you with the article in her mouth, give support to her jaw to keep her from dropping the article, and gently guide her into a *sit* position. Remove the article and replace it with a treat. Repeat this many times until your **puppy** is proficient in performing the command.

Use your inventiveness to further your **puppy's** mastery of the word *bring.* If you have a helper, sit on opposite sides of a room, and take turns giving the command to Brandy. Each time, after you reward her, just ask her to *hold* it, and wait for

51

the helper to call her. It is particularly important that you always require that your **puppy** assume a *sit* position and that she holds the article until you take it. This results in an extremely attractive delivery.

Once you've succeeded in teaching Brandy the first four of the secondary commands, give her the following test. This will indicate where Brandy needs some more practice. Place an article 20 feet (6 m) away, give these commands in sequence, and make the necessary corrections.

1. **Brandy,** *go get* **it.**

2. **Brandy,** *sit* **and** *hold* **it.**

3. **Brandy,** *drop* **it.**

4. **Brandy,** *get* **it.**

5. **Brandy,** *down* **and** *hold* **it.**

6. **Brandy,** *come bring* **it.**

The Word Up

The fifth secondary command for Brandy to learn is the word *up.* The word *up* will be used for positioning her above the floor, the ground, or a particular level. You will be able to direct her *up* on couches and beds, into truck cabs, up stairs, etc. Please note that the *up* command does not refer to the action of jumping but to your **puppy's** positioning herself above the level she's on. In Chapter 12, you will have the option of using the command *jump* for the purpose of directing Brandy to jump over anything specified. The word *up* will increase her vocabulary when you use it in the following sentences:

1. **Brandy,** *go up.*

2. **Brandy,** *go up* **and** *get* **it.**

3. Brandy, *go up* and *drop* it.

4. Brandy, *come up.*

Brandy will catch on quickly to the word *up* because it will usually mean a reward for her. Getting up on the couch with you is a privilege, and extremely comfortable too! **Puppies will be eager for the opportunity to climb into the family car. Some will like the comfort, some the view, and others will appreciate not being left behind. For training, it will be helpful if you allow Brandy *up* on at least one chair in the house. In our family we have designated a "dog chair" on which the dogs can use whenever they wish. They love their privilege and respect the other furniture in the house. If you are a new dog owner and haven't started a furniture policy yet, I suggest that your dogs shouldn't be allowed up on anything without your direct command.**

Start the training for the word *up* by having Brandy sit facing a chair approximately 2 feet (.6 m) away. Have your treats ready and stand behind the chair so that the chair is between you and your puppy. Give the command, "Brandy, *come up*," while patting the cushion of the chair. When she jumps up, quickly help her into a comfortable position and reward her. This should be easy for most puppies. Initially they will respond more to the hand signal of patting the cushion. If Brandy has difficulty, it's probably because of your previous training regarding the furniture. Try to entice her with food. Help her up into the chair, if necessary, while showering praise on her. Be patient and keep everything positive and happy. She'll catch on.

As soon as she is responding to "Brandy, *come up*," start increasing her distance away from the chair before you give the command. Then proceed by not patting the chair anymore. Now back up a few feet in a line with Brandy and the chair and try it again. Continue the practice, backing up each time. Remember to reward her each time she succeeds. Take it

step by step. If she gets confused, repeat the previous steps. You might want to use different chairs. Or try sitting on a couch when you give the command. In the future when you call your puppy upstairs, give the command, "Brandy, *come up*." You'll find it will even help Brandy to locate you.

Now that your puppy has learned "Brandy, *come up*," it is time to teach her the "Brandy, *go up*" command. Position her and yourself a few feet in front of a chair. Give the command, take a step forward, pat the chair, and reward her when she gets up on the chair. Increase the distance slowly and continue, traveling quickly to the chair with her each time. Decrease the patting of the chair each time until the patting of the chair is unnecessary. Next, instead of traveling to the chair, allow your hand to swing out toward the chair as you give the command. If your puppy is slow to respond, quickly run toward the chair, directing her. Soon she'll get it!

As soon as your puppy understands the word *up,* experiment with the sentences, "Brandy, *go up* and *drop* it," and "Brandy, *go up* and *get it*." Both should be easy for your puppy because she understands the components of the command. Merely help her through it a few times, making the necessary corrections. Remember to keep things incredibly positive by using frequent praise.

Have your puppy *sit* at your side, hand her a favorite article, and say, "Brandy, *hold* it." Use the same chair and the same spot as in the *up* training. Give the command, "Brandy, *go up* and *drop* it." Initially put a lot of emphasis on the "Brandy, *go up*" portion of the command. If your puppy drops the article on the way up, quickly put it back in her mouth, pause, and tell her to *hold* it. If your puppy succeeds in jumping up while holding on to the article but fails to drop it, remain silent. The reason for the silence is to tell her that her mission is not finished yet. During this silence, puppies will either drop the article, as you requested, or hold it, awaiting

54

your instructions. If necessary, repeat the "*drop* it," praise her thoroughly, and repeat the exercise. If your **puppy** is having problems, stop the exercise and go back to practicing the elements of the *hold* and *up* commands. It's important that she doesn't get a negative feeling for the command. Go slowly enough to allow her to succeed.

To teach your **puppy** the command, "Brandy, *go up* and *get it*," start a playing session with her favorite toy. Once she is in an excited state, quickly put her in a *sit-stay,* and throw the toy to the rear of the seat of the practice chair. Give the command, but make sure she doesn't grab the article without jumping up on to the chair first. A strong "No!" will work if she reaches for it. This should be followed by repeating the full command. As soon as she jumps up, direct her to get it. You probably won't need to give the command, "Brandy, *come bring* it." Your **puppy** will quickly return to the playing session with her toy. Play a bit and try it again.

The four sentences that I've introduced you to are the most practical. You will be able to use the word *up* in combination with other words you have taught thus far. I haven't mentioned them, because it's usually more successful to direct Brandy *up* with one command and then follow it with any other command you might desire. You will notice that *up* is always used with the major directives *go* or *come*. The reason for this is that the word *up* always implies a necessary movement to a particular level.

The Word Nose
The last of the secondary commands is the word *nose.* The training for this word is found in Chapter 3. If Brandy is not presently nosing a bell to communicate her needs, then review Chapter 3. Don't proceed with the following exercises until Brandy has mastered nosing the bells. Once understood, the *nose* command can be used for other purposes. You can have fun directing her to open or close doors or drawers and to retrieve large balls or similar objects that she can't grab.

The word *nose* will be added to Brandy's vocabulary when you use it in the following sentences:

1. Brandy, *nose* it.

2. Brandy, *go nose* it.

3. Brandy, *come nose* it.

Select the proper sentence based on the movement required of your **puppy**. To avoid confusion, don't conduct advanced nose training near the bells. You may use treats as rewards in this advanced work but remember to be patient and take it step by step. Use the same methods that you used on the bell, and your progress will be assured.

The secondary commands you've learned in this chapter will widen your range of control over your puppy. Allowing Brandy to be helpful will increase her happiness and even save you steps. You should require that she pick up after herself. Have her place her toys in her toy box when they're not in use. If you see an item on the floor or couch that needs to be thrown away, direct her to do it for you. If you need the morning paper, your slippers, or even her brush, your puppy can easily be trained to accommodate you. If you sleep with your door closed at night, allow her to close it for you. Permit her to help you daily

and reward her for it. It's a sure way to increase your mutual love and happiness.

The First Fifteen Magic Words

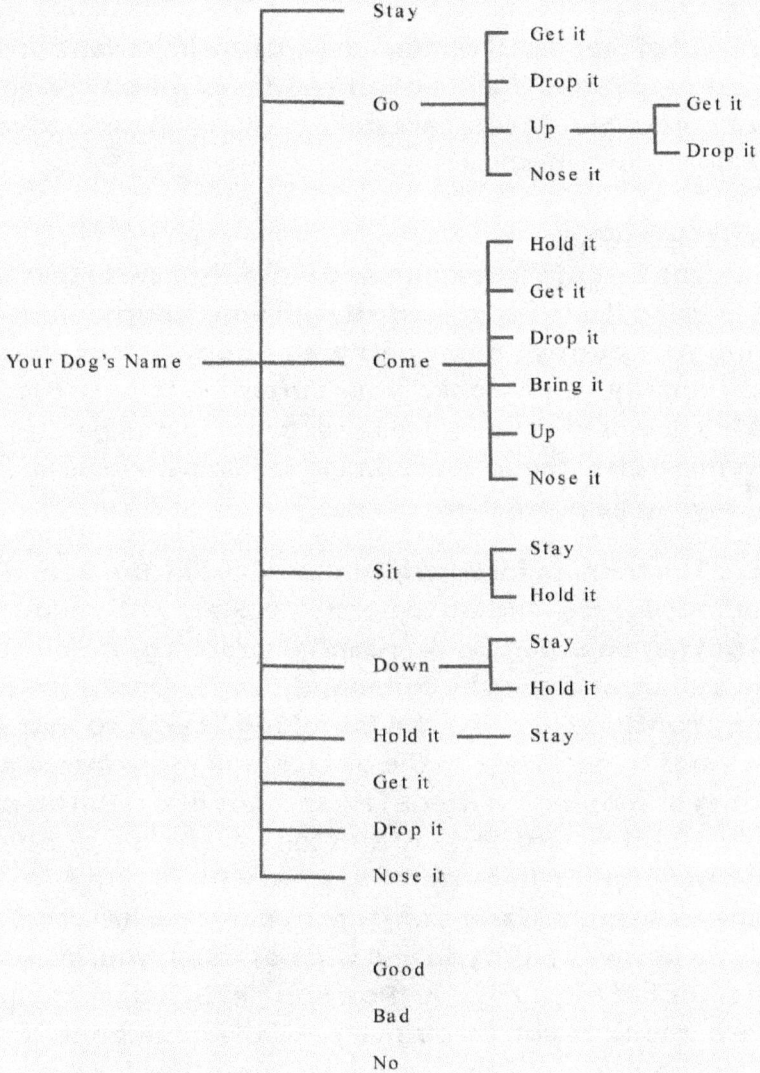

```
                                          ┌─── Stay
                                          │
                                          │              ┌─── Get it
                                          │              │
                                          │              ├─── Drop it              ┌─── Get it
                                          │      Go ─────┤                         │
                                          │              ├─── Up ──────────────────┤
                                          │              │                         └─── Drop it
                                          │              └─── Nose it
                                          │
                                          │              ┌─── Hold it
                                          │              │
                                          │              ├─── Get it
                                          │              │
                                          │              ├─── Drop it
    Your Dog's Name ─────────────────────┤      Come ───┤
                                          │              ├─── Bring it
                                          │              │
                                          │              ├─── Up
                                          │              │
                                          │              └─── Nose it
                                          │
                                          │                     ┌─── Stay
                                          │      Sit ───────────┤
                                          │                     └─── Hold it
                                          │
                                          │                     ┌─── Stay
                                          │      Down ──────────┤
                                          │                     └─── Hold it
                                          │
                                          ├─── Hold it ──── Stay
                                          │
                                          ├─── Get it
                                          │
                                          ├─── Drop it
                                          │
                                          └─── Nose it


                                   Good

                                   Bad

                                   No
```

#10 Special Commands: Look, Bark, Walk, Okay and Hurry

All of the special command words are important, practical, and serve to make the life of you and your **puppy** easier and more enjoyable. Several are necessary for the effective use of your **puppy**'s new language.

The Word Look

The first of these command words is *look*. In teaching it and in using it, always precede it with your **puppy**'s name. Saying your **puppy**'s name gets your **puppy** to look at you. When you say, "Lady, look," your purpose is to keep her looking at you until you release her or command her to do something else. The *look* command is also beneficial in introducing new material.

The training for *look* is remarkably like the training you gave Lady for responding to her name. Start with a food reward and put her on a *stay*. Walk around the room, grab something from a shelf, and give the command, "Lady, *look*." Praise your **puppy** continually while she is looking at you, so that she continues to do so. Make the object look more interesting by turning or moving it. After a few seconds of her full attention, throw a food reward her way and tell her she is a *good* dog. You can lengthen her attention span with practice. You might try using different objects to keep her interest fresh. If Lady turns away from you and will not watch you, make it easier for her to watch you. Position her in a dark room and have her look at you through a partially open door. If you are still having trouble, use a more tempting food reward and more interesting objects, such as a new squeaky toy or a steak bone. You shouldn't have much of a problem teaching the word *look* to her. Remember to lengthen her attention span slowly, allowing her to succeed each time. The clap hand signal can also be used with this command. You will be introduced to it in Chapter 12.

The Word Bark

The seventeenth word in the language is the word *bark.* Though you might think it difficult to teach the *bark* command to Lady, I assure you it's not. Almost every **puppy** barks naturally. All that's needed is to train her to do it on command. I recommend this word to all dog owners for the added security the command provides as well as for enhancing their dog's personality. In your home a dog's bark is usually enough to make a potential intruder try somewhere else. Even if the dog sounds small, the intruder won't want to mess with an alarm device equipped with teeth. If you are out late at night walking your dog and see some not-so-neighborly-looking characters approaching, it's useful to whisper the *bark* command to your dog and have her begin barking. I would then cross the street, keeping an eye on the strangers, or walk to a well-lit house with my barking dog. If the individuals you are passing in the night are law-abiding citizens, they will appreciate your avoiding them!

Lady's personality can be enhanced when she learns to bark on command. Though a bark is a sharp, loud vocal expression, it can be a beautiful sound to you. This is **especially true if Lady barks only when she hears noises or upon your request. The encouragement of your puppy's vocal abilities will lead to other sounds. Howls, little woofs, moans, or whimpers can easily be obtained from your puppy by rewarding her each time she gives you the sound. A talking dog has more character!**

You can add the word *bark* to Lady's vocabulary by using it in the following sentences:

1. **Lady,** *bark.*

2. **Lady,** *go bark.*

3. Lady, *come bark.*

The first sentence, "Lady, *bark,*" is used when an immediate vocal response is desired. The major directives *go* and *come* are combined with the *bark* when movement is needed. These two sentences can be used in the home for protection. If you and Lady are watching television and you hear a noise in the kitchen, send her to check it out, using the command, "Lady, *go bark.*" Soon she will understand which noises she should be concerned with. If she is asleep in another room, and you hear a strange sound, call her with, "Lady, *come bark.*" If there is possible danger, you'll want her on the job.

To teach Lady to bark on command, it is necessary that you use a stimulant that makes her bark. Try to duplicate situations in which your puppy will bark naturally, then praise her for it. If possible, stop her barking by gently holding her muzzle. Then release it and give her the *bark* command. Reward her with a treat and repeat the exercise. Often, if you make a barking sound or Lady hears another dog bark, she will bark also. Dogs often bark out of fear of the unknown.

With the help of a friend or another member of the family, a variety of situations can be set up. First, it is best to trick Lady into thinking that only you and she are in the house. Have everybody else leave for a period. Your helper can either sneak into a back room or stay outside the house. Ask your helper to make strange noises by pounding on the side of the house, scratching at the door, or playing strange voices from your cell phone. Your helper should make noises until Lady barks. When she stops, the helper should wait for about twenty seconds before repeating the noise. This will reward Lady for her barking, since she will think that her barking stopped the intruder. Whenever you are in the house with Lady and hear a sound, adopt a worried expression, and tell her to *bark.* Run to the area of the noise as you praise her for barking. When she has barked a couple times, hand her a treat. This will reward her further and keep her from overreacting to a small noise. A good guard dog will bark a bit and then stop to listen for additional noises. A Halloween mask viewed through a window may provoke Lady to bark. When she barks, the person wearing the mask should pretend to be scared and leave.

In these setup situations it is best not to **let** Lady know that the stranger is a friend of hers. This can be accomplished easily by asking that your helper delay entering the **house** for five minutes. Specify **in** advance that your helper repeat the noise cycle a certain number of times and then quit. This way both of you will know when the **training** has ended. Wait with Lady and listen in silence. Afterward, play with her as a final reward. Work daily on the *bark* command until you can whisper it and get an appropriate and **immediate** response. (Depending upon the circumstance, it might sometimes be wise to inform your neighbors of your training plans. Otherwise, they might call the police to **investigate** your intruder.)

The Word Walk

The word *walk* pertains to **Lady's** daily constitutional for exercise and the excretion of waste. Even if you have a backyard to let her use for this purpose, the need for walking her may arise when you are at Aunt Martha's house, playing in a city park, or on a summer vacation. The word *walk* will need little work before your **puppy** understands it. The real training will be in controlling the walk. Public pressure requires you to walk your **puppy** in suitable places. A **puppy** that can walk **in** a designated area can be taken anywhere with confidence.

Let's say that you have an errand to run **in** town. Always ask yourself the following questions before taking Lady with you:

1. Is the errand a **long** one or a quick stop?

2. If you must leave **her in the car, will it be too** hot for her, or will she be **in danger of being stolen?**

3. If you can't **leave her in the car, is** there an area just inside or outside the building where you can *down* her and watch her?

4. If you plan to enter the building with your **puppy**, does the building have tenants or a guard who might object?

5. Do you **have everything you need with you - - a leash,** water, bags for her waste, and some rewards?

6. Will your trip **take** so long that it will be necessary to walk her?

7. Will there be a suitable place to walk her?

If your answer to question six is yes, then you need **to** answer question seven with a yes. **If you think** you might have trouble finding a suitable place to give **her** a walk at your destination, stop at an appropriate spot before you get there. Never take her for a walk in someone else's yard, in front of an office building, or anywhere where **there** are many people. Pick areas such as an empty field or the edge of a parking **lot** that is full of weeds. These areas are less likely to offend anyone and of course, pick up any deposit.

The word *walk* can be used in the following sentences:

1. Lady, *walk?*

2. Lady, *go walk.*

3. Lady, *come walk.*

The first sentence is a question that you may ask your **puppy**. Different **puppies** will react differently. By their reaction to your question, you'll be able to gauge how immediate their need is. Some will look at you sadly or begin crying, others will get excited and start jumping around. If Lady is at home, she can use the bell to tell you. But when she is out with you, the question comes in handy. Remember to change the tone of your voice on the word *walk* to signify a question.

The sentence, "Lady, *go walk*," is used both for permission and direction. You're telling her that it is all right to relieve herself in the area you're directing her to. Approach the area, stop on the perimeter facing the center of the walk area, and give the command.

The sentence, "Lady, *come walk*," can be used in two ways. The first is when your position is between Lady and the walk area. Here you give your **puppy** permission to pass you and *walk*. The second way is when she has traveled toward the outside perimeter of a *walk* area and is ready to relieve herself in an inappropriate area. In this case giving the command will move Lady's sniffing toward you and into the proper area.

The word *walk* is an important word to your **puppy**. The training involves controlling the when and where of the *walk*. It requires daily practice until sufficient control is reached, then occasional review to maintain it. Even if you have a large backyard, and it's convenient and easy to let Lady out in the mornings, don't. Get dressed, then head out the front door with Lady on her leash. Mornings are perfect for the initial practice because it's a sure thing that Lady needs a *walk*.

Find a suitable spot for the walk. A restricted area is best at first. If possible, pick one that has two clear borders (a fence and a sidewalk). Your full attention should be given to Lady, so avoid distractions and practice control. Snap off the leash, if there is no danger for your **puppy**, and give Lady permission by saying, "Lady, *go walk*." If she approaches the border of the desired area, give a strong "No!" then give the command, "Lady, *come walk*." Initially she might test you and not listen. If she doesn't obey, run to her, stop her in her quest for relief, and snap the leash back on. Return to your original position on the border, and make Lady *sit* at your side for a few seconds. Then release her by saying again, "Lady, *go walk*." Although this may seem like a lengthy procedure, it is necessary to teach her that she must listen to you especially if she wants that walk. Praise her for using the proper area.

Daily practice for two weeks will give Lady the control she needs. If possible, try a different area each day. Some should be large areas with no borders; others should be small areas of gravel, weeds, or grass. The large borderless areas are the hard ones. Here you must make imaginary borders and stick to them. If you don't, your **puppy** can travel far and get out of your range of control, chase another dog, or sniff a scared passerby. Take Lady for a walk in the afternoon and evening when she nudges the bell. This will give you a chance to show her that the *walk* must be controlled then, too.

The *walk* should also be practiced on a leash. This may be awkward for you and unnatural for your **puppy**. But after a while, both of you will get accustomed to it. Local laws may require that you use a leash, but even where they don't, it can be good practice. The training in giving the *walk* command on a leash will be valuable if you must walk your **puppy** in a place where there are a lot of people or traffic and her safety is endangered.

Although your **puppy**'s need to relieve herself is simply a need of nature, it can be embarrassing. If you attain good control of your **puppy** and are careful to select the best *walk* spots you can, it will be less embarrassing. Speed up the whole process so you attract as little attention as possible. The twentieth "magic" word, *hurry,* will be a big help to you in doing this.

The Word Okay

The last two words in Lady's twenty-word vocabulary are the words *okay* and *hurry.* These words share common ground in that they are two-syllable words. I mentioned the importance of confining Lady's vocabulary to one-syllable words. Using only one-syllable words simplifies the language and avoids much confusion. The words *okay* and *hurry* are allowed as exceptions because they are always used by themselves. These words are not to be used together or in combination with other words that would result in confusion for your **puppy**. *Okay* and *hurry* are also the best and the most natural words to use for the purpose that they fulfill.

The word *okay* is used as a release command. It gives Lady the approval to break a *stay* or, if you're involved in a training session, it dismisses her to play, sleep, chase birds, or whatever she wishes to do. In using *okay,* your tone of voice will be important. It should sound both happy and excited.

Care should be taken not to use *good* as a release word or *okay* for praise. Keep their meanings and their uses separate. Always correct Lady if she breaks a *stay* on the word *good*. *Good* implies doing the proper thing; it is not permission to play. Refer to Chapter 6 for a review of the word *good*. If *okay* is accidentally used as a praise word, it can put Lady's safety in jeopardy. Let us say that you're on a busy street corner and for some reason you've forgotten your leash. Using the word *okay* at this time instead of *good* could lead to a disastrous break in her control. Never use *okay* or, for that matter, anything other than a whisper of *good* when you're in a situation that might be dangerous.

A release word or signal is an important part of Lady's vocabulary. Without it she will eventually disobey you and release herself, and you can't blame her. It is impossible to give Lady the option of releasing herself and still maintain control over her. You'll find the word *okay* easy to use and effective in properly releasing your **puppy** from a *stay* or a training session. Remember that an implied *stay* also needs a release. If you have downed Lady next to you, don't allow her to move until you release her. She will quickly understand that *okay* means that she is on her own. Just be consistent in its use.

The Word Hurry

The twentieth magic word is *hurry.* This word demands an immediate response. The command is given in an enthusiastic tone conveying eagerness and urgency. Rule 10 in Chapter 4 says that you should give a command only once. If you repeat a command, you are teaching Lady that she doesn't have to listen to you the first time. The word *hurry* is a safety valve that keeps you from repeating the original command and tells Lady to hasten in obeying it. You'll be amazed when she completes the assigned task after ignoring the command so completely that you'd swear she never heard it.

There is not much training involved in teaching the word *hurry.* It's more a matter of your learning how and when to use it. The word *hurry* is used by itself and doesn't follow your **puppy**'s name. Use it when Lady is slow in responding to a command or when she doesn't respond at all. You can use it after a command containing the major directive *go* or *come* and whenever a *get* or *nose* is used. Other commands are tricky, and you need a feeling for their use. You have two basic alternatives in correcting either a slow response or no response: Make a correction or use the word *hurry.* Use your judgment about making a physical correction, depending on the situation. If you are in a public place or among friends at home, I wouldn't make a correction unless it's a behavior problem involving a stranger or friend. Commands like *sit, down,* and *drop* imply no major movement, so you don't want to wait all day for a simple request. Here a correction or possibly a review of the training involved in the command would be in order.

When Lady has mastered the special commands, she has acquired Twenty Magic Words. *Look, bark,* and *walk* are helpful words in making life easier and more enjoyable for both you and her. Since you will always release her after giving her certain commands, you will be using the word *okay* frequently. *Hurry* is a command that will speed her on her way to carrying out a previous command. The continuous use of the commands and careful

The Twenty Magic Words

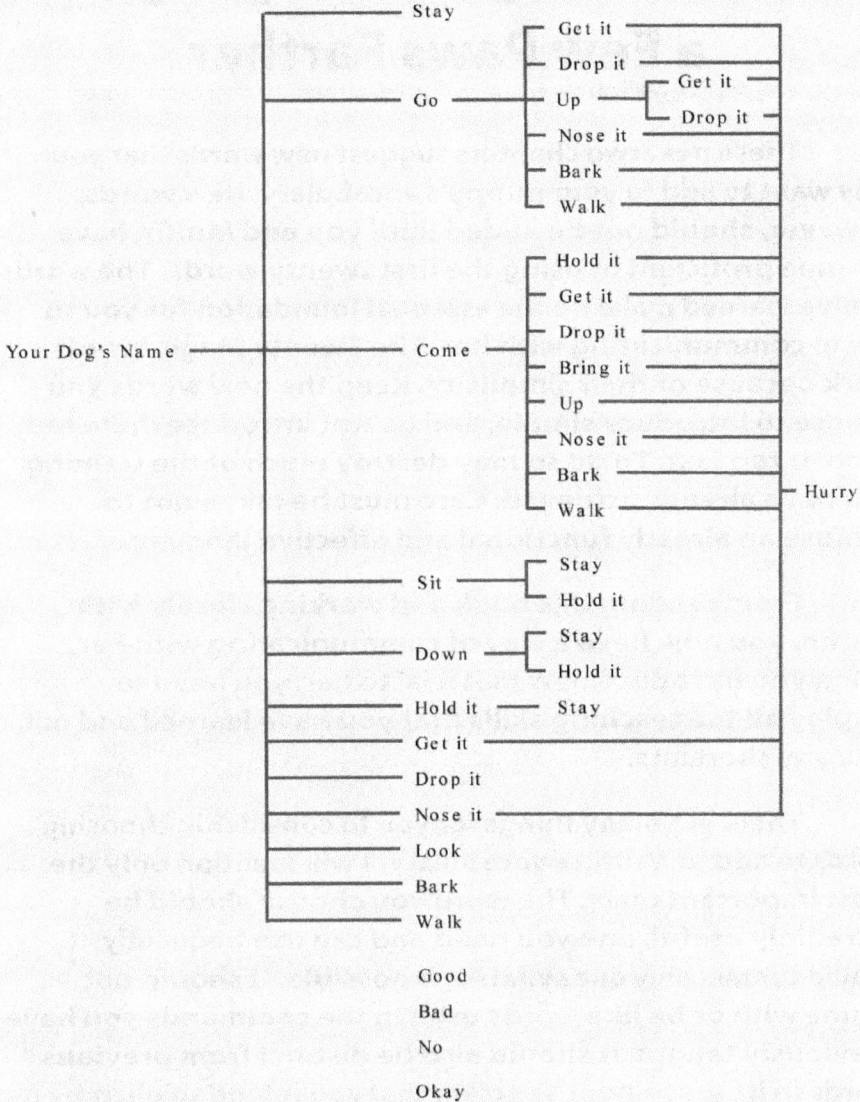

Your Dog's Name
- Stay
- Go
  - Get it
  - Drop it
  - Up
    - Get it
    - Drop it
  - Nose it
  - Bark
  - Walk
- Come
  - Hold it
  - Get it
  - Drop it
  - Bring it
  - Up
  - Nose it
  - Bark
  - Walk
- Sit
  - Stay
  - Hold it
- Down
  - Stay
  - Hold it
- Hold it — Stay
- Get it
- Drop it
- Nose it
- Look
- Bark
- Walk

Hurry

Good

Bad

No

Okay

observation of the rules in Chapter 4 will allow your puppy to maintain her understanding of the language and help her in expanding her vocabulary.

#11 Taking the Language a Few Paws Farther

These next two chapters suggest new words that you may want to add to your puppy's vocabulary. New words, however, should not be added until you and Muffin have become proficient in using the first twenty words. The words you've learned make up the essential foundation for you to use in communicating with her. The Twenty Magic Words work because of their simplicity. Keep the new words you choose to introduce simple, and do not introduce them too soon or too fast. To do so may destroy much of the training you have already achieved. Care must be taken not to confuse an already functional and effective language.

From reading this book and working closely with Muffin, you now have a way of communicating with her. When you introduce new material to her, you need to employ all the teaching skills that you have learned and not take any shortcuts.

There are many things for you to consider in choosing words to add to Muffin's vocabulary. I will mention only the most important ones. The word you choose should be incredibly useful, one you need and can use frequently. It should contain only one syllable, if possible. It should not rhyme with or be like words used in the commands you have previously taught. It should also be distinct from previous words in its meaning. The action that you intend to elicit by its use should be distinct from the actions you have been able to obtain with any previous commands. Be sure to consider your choice of new words with care. You will not want them to interfere with or undo any of the previous training you have achieved.

Categories of New Words

First, I will cover some of the general categories of possible new words you may wish to introduce. These categories will include different groups of words that might be useful to you. A basic guide to the training involved will also be included.

Names of Persons

If you teach Muffin the names of the members of your household, you will not only be able to direct her to each one but also to make deliveries to them. Just think how convenient it will be when Dad calls from upstairs for a screwdriver or Mom wants your dirty shirt to wash.

All these situations are easily handled by using the major directive *go* in combination with the person's name. Just hand Muffin the object or message. Say, "Muffin, *go* to Joey," and send her off in the right direction to find him. The requested delivery should always be followed with a cookie when your puppy returns to you. Start Muffin's habit of returning to you by calling her after the delivery is made. That way your puppy will receive oral praise at her destination, return to you quickly for a cookie, and be ready for another delivery. It should be obvious how much fun your puppy or dog will have doing this.

To teach your puppy to differentiate between different people's names, initially train her to travel to the designated person without an item to deliver. Upon arrival, have the person reward her with a cookie and praise her. Sharpen Muffin's knowledge further by having two of the people she knows stand on the other side of the room from you and her. Send Muffin to a specific person, who should praise her when she arrives. If she goes to the wrong person, that person should not react at all. Then, repeat the command until Muffin finds the right person. You will find that your puppy will pick it up quickly.

69

Names of Places

Words signifying certain places can also be particularly useful in Muffin's vocabulary. If you desire to send **her** away from you, it will be helpful to specify where you wish her to *go*. The place words **that** you may wish to teach her without bogging down the language are *"wall," "door," "stairs," "bed,"* and *"house." "Wall"* is any upright structure that divides or encloses; *"door"* refers to the doorway of a room; *"stairs"* are a series of steps between **levels**; *"bed"* is the area or the pad where Muffin sleeps at night; and *"house"* refers to **her** doghouse if she has one. These words are not applicable to all dogs. Some dogs won't have houses, and others will have no reason to know what a doorway is. One of our dogs enjoys lying at the door and guarding the entrance.

All these words are used in combination with the major directive *go*. An example would be, "Muffin, *go* to *bed*." Begin training her by starting close to the place you want her to go. Then give the command, run her over to that place, and reward her. Once Muffin does it on her own, increase the distance between the starting place and where you want her to *go*. **This** method should work easily for all places except *"stairs." "Stairs"* will be discussed later in this chapter.

Compound commands should be delayed until Muffin has mastered the new words suggested in this chapter. A compound command is a sentence such as, "Muffin, *go* to the *wall* and *drop* it," or "Muffin, *go* to the *door* and *bark*." For the time being it is best to limit your command to sending her to a certain place and then giving her a separate command after she gets there.

Names of Objects

You may want to include in Muffin's vocabulary the names of a few objects that you will use frequently. Some of the names that I find useful are the names of my dogs' hairbrush, certain of their toys, and their favorite foods. The hairbrush is simply "*brush*;" the toys have simple but distinctive names such as "*chew*," "*squeaky*," "*sock*," and "*ball*;" and the several food items have names such as "*cookie*," or "*steak*."

To teach Muffin to *get* her brush, for instance, I would say, "Muffin, *go get* the *brush*." Then with hand signals I would guide her to the brush, call it again by its name, and help her pick it up. After rewarding her with praise, I would gradually increase the distance between the brush and the place where I give the command. I have found it convenient to keep her brush in an open shoe box on the closet floor. This provides a good drop zone for the brush's return. Though it's hard for me to brush my dog daily, allowing her to get the brush and put it away helps me to get the occasional grooming done.

Requesting certain toys can keep the play session interesting. To teach Muffin the names of several of her toys, get her to look at one of her toys while you say the name of the toy. When you have done this for two of the toys, place them a distance apart on the open floor. Then use a command like, "Muffin, *go get* the *ball*" and guide her to the ball. Gradually guide her less and less. Command her to get the other toy, guiding her to it at first. Then alternate your command to get the ball or the other toy. Eventually you can introduce a third toy and maybe a fourth toy.

The name-dropping of a favorite food can be used to increase the excitement for an upcoming training session. After a couple of minutes of anticipation, grab the food item and begin the training. Teaching Muffin the name of her favorite foods is rather easy. She will learn quickly if you say the name of what you are giving her each time you reward her.

Tricks

You can add words to Muffin's vocabulary that direct her to carry out special tricks. Some examples of these are

71

paw, shake, bow, crawl, and *roll.* Try to limit your commands to one word.

To get her to roll over, use the word *roll,* not the phrase "*roll* over." An exception might be in trying to make her look even smarter. For example, instead of asking Muffin for her paw, ask for a specific paw and teach her the difference between the commands *left paw* and *right paw.* Your friends will think you have the smartest **puppy** in the neighborhood!

Tricks will be limited only by your imagination. When training your **puppy** to do a trick, it is necessary to proceed step by step and to reward her as she succeeds in accomplishing each step. For instance, a crawl is easily achieved by first giving her the command, "Muffin, *down.*" With a piece of food in your hand, tempt her to stretch forward for it. Use your other hand to gently keep her in the *down* position if she attempts to get up. Allow her to succeed in reaching the food but require her to reach a little farther each time. Tapping the floor with the food works well as a hand signal. The *come* command can help in communicating to Muffin that she should move toward you for the food. In the crawl, she needs to shift her front paws to move forward and scoot her hindquarters along. If necessary, you can help her by moving one paw at a time so that she gets the idea and the food reward.

Vocal Sounds

If your **puppy** makes a variety of vocal sounds, words can be added to his or her language to define them. The vocal expressions possible are "little woof," "cry," "moan," "howl," "bark," and "growl." I recommend teaching your **puppy** the word associated with the vocal noise, unless it happens to be "cry" or "growl." I caution you here because a crying **puppy** is very annoying to most people, and a growling **puppy** can sound extremely dangerous, and growling shouldn't be encouraged. The bark of a dog is sufficient for the sake of protection.

A talking **puppy** has an enriched personality compared with one that doesn't talk. Strongly encourage Muffin whenever she makes a sound that you'd **like** to hear more often. This often happens when a puppy yawns. Once Muffin is making that sound **often**, associate a word to describe it while you praise **her**. In your **training** sessions, ask Muffin **to** make the sound while tempting her with a piece of food. Often mimicking the sound will help. If your **puppy** is trying hard but no sound comes out, you might want to reward her efforts. Have patience. It can take a lot of encouragement for Muffin to make a particular vocal sound.

Although I **love** talking dogs, I should mention a problem associated with them. A great talker can interrupt conversations and phone calls. In case you have overtaught the vocal sounds, and your little friend has become a constant gabber and interrupts you, the command word *quiet* can be used. Initially, you will have to teach Muffin the **meaning** of the word by using a squirt bottle of water. Give Muffin the oral command, "Quiet!" If she talks, give her one squirt, and reinforce the command *quiet.* Praise her for being quiet and be prepared for another correction. She'll pick up the meaning quickly.

I remind you to wait to add new words, until you and Muffin have become proficient in using the first twenty words. The words you've learned make up the essential foundation for you to use in communicating with her. Care must be taken not to confuse an already functional and effective language.

#12 Other Helpful Words

This chapter is concerned with ten valuable words that can be added to Muffin's vocabulary. Though these words fit into one of the general categories previously mentioned, their possible existence and importance easily could be overlooked. These words can be especially useful and deserve the extra explanation given.

The Word Back

The word *back* is used to move Muffin backward. If her placement is a bit too far forward, move her back. This will happen when Muffin crowds you too closely, when she's in danger of being accidentally stepped on by less aware company, or as a correction when you command her *down* but she takes an extra step toward you. The command *back* is used in conjunction with Muffin's name or by itself, depending on her attention.

To teach Muffin to *back,* find or create a narrow passageway that will prevent her from turning around. This can be done by placing three chairs in a hallway to make it narrower or by pulling a bed close enough to a wall. Just leave enough room for her width, no matter how broad your beam has become.

You'll be teaching Muffin by using a hand signal for *back.* This signal is remarkably like the *stay* hand signal in that the palm of your fully opened hand is facing her. In the *back* hand signal, though, the hand pushes back and forth toward her nose.

First, put Muffin in the passageway, say the oral command, and use the hand signal at her eye level. While giving the hand signal, allow your palm to come up to Muffin's nose and push gently. This should cause Muffin to move backward. Shower praise on her, or even give her a food reward, and then repeat the exercise. As you practice, slowly

74

widen the passageway until Muffin can execute the command in a completely open area such as your living room. If she begins to turn around instead of backing up at your command, return to practicing in a narrow passageway again.

For backing up a long distance I prefer using the hand signal to the oral command, so that I don't have to repeat the oral command several times. Just say the oral command to get Muffin's attention and follow it by using the hand signal until she has backed far enough. For showing-off purposes, it's more spectacular to have her *back* up in whatever body position she is in when you ask her to *back* up. If she is in a *down* position, she should *back* up in a *down* position. If she is in a *sit* position, she should back up and remain in a *sit* position.

The Word Catch

The word *catch* alerts Muffin to the fact that you are going to throw something to her and that you intend that she catch it. Having her catch a food reward can greatly reduce the time of training sessions and save you steps in rewarding her. The quicker you praise or correct, the sooner your training will convey the intended message (see Chapter 4, Rule 8). Quickly tossing a food reward is as immediate as you can get.

Puppies vary greatly in their natural ability to catch things, but all puppies can be trained to do better than they would without training. Training involves throwing small pieces of food to Muffin. Command her to *down* about five feet (1.5 m) away from you and toss a piece of food to her. Keep your tosses gentle, and initially aim at Muffin's mouth. When she succeeds in catching almost everyone, angle your throws slightly to the side. Increase the challenge as Muffin improves. Build her catching ability slowly, always allowing her to catch more than she misses by adjusting the difficulty of your throws.

Typically, Muffin's attention will be on you when you

are about to toss her a toy or a bite of food. Both are rewards that will arouse her interest and hold her attention. In this case, just say, "*Catch*!" and make the toss. Muffin will learn the word *catch* quickly because she will know that something enjoyable is coming her way - - by air mail. If Muffin's attention is not on you when you want her to catch something, use her name first, followed by the word *catch*.

The *catch* command carries with it a certain trust that must never be broken. You ask her to catch only those items that are completely and safely catchable. Her eyesight limits her ability to discern whether it's a rock or a piece of food. Build her trust in you by being as faithful to her as she is to you.

The Word Eat

The word *eat* refers to Muffin's natural ability to devour food. It is used in conjunction with *go* or *come* to direct her to eat, depending on your relative position. In Chapter 4, Rule 13, I explained how helpful it is to put Muffin through a short training session before you allow her to eat. The word *eat* is used to release Muffin from the training session to go eat. You should give the *eat* command as a reward only after she has performed well. To train Muffin to understand the new word *eat*, simply say the command, and run with her to her food. It is the easiest word you'll ever teach her!

The Word Heel

The *heel* command requires Muffin to travel along at your left side. In the *heel* position Muffin must always be aware of your speed, direction, and possible changes in either. Similarly, you should constantly be aware that she is with you and accentuate your style of walking to make it possible for her to always maintain the *heel* position. When you change the gait of the walk, making directional changes, or even stop completely, you should give Muffin a chance to sense that a change is coming. This is accomplished by slowing down slightly and thus signaling to your puppy to be ready to adjust accordingly. If you make a left turn, for example, you should slow down, make the turn, and accelerate slowly to your normal speed. If you don't slow down, you might find yourself tripping over your loyal and honorable companion. Before coming to a complete stop, you should gradually slow down and then stop. On stopping, Muffin should assume a *sit* position directly at your side.

If you are serious about teaching Muffin to *heel*, I would suggest that you seek professional help in your vicinity. Dog trainers generally specialize in this area and spend their whole lives helping people to train their dogs. Obedience training classes cover heeling, staying, jumping, retrieving, sitting, and lying down. For training purposes, the classes present many advantages. You will have the guidance of a professional trainer, your commitment will force you to take your **puppy** out at least once a week, and the school will have distractions that you don't usually have at home. The distractions usually consist of other people and dogs. You can be sure that when Muffin learns despite all the distractions, she will be able to carry out your commands when you and she come home. You'll like the trainer and the people you meet in the classes, since you all have an interest in common - - your love of dogs.

A dog that knows how to *heel* commands much respect in the community and can go almost anywhere. People will love your dog because they see few that are so well behaved and under control. A mugger would think twice before approaching a woman with a dog heeling at her side. Why should the mugger take a chance when the dog obviously has been well trained! If you train Muffin to *heel*, you will take her out more often and go to more places. Your life and your dog's life will be enriched because of it.

The Word Jump

The word *up* (see Chapter 9) directs Muffin to attain something at a higher level and to stay there. The word *jump* refers to your **puppy**'s springing or leaping. Use the word *up* if you don't care how Muffin attains the higher level. Use the words *jump up* if you want her to leap up on something, rather than crawling up or walking up. Use the word *jump* when you require Muffin to leap over an object and return to the same level.

You can teach Muffin to jump by placing a stick on top of blocks at about half her height. Start by positioning it in a doorway or narrow passageway. Stay on one side, and command her into a *sit* position on the other side. Then give the command, "Muffin, *come jump* it," as you back away from the stick. If you haven't placed the stick too high, it will be natural for her to jump over it to come to you. Continue to raise the height of the stick, and she will learn to jump higher and higher. A healthy **puppy** should be able to jump over things that are at least one-and-a-half times her shoulder height.

Once Muffin has learned to jump proficiently in the restricted doorway or passageway, place the stick and blocks in an open area. Then start all over again with the stick at lower levels. Teach Muffin to jump over various objects like a large cushion, fallen branches and even kid sister Susie.

Later you can train your **puppy** to respond to the command, "Muffin, *go jump* it." Always be sure to use the full command - - her name, the major directive *go* or *come*, and the words *jump* it. Also be sure to give Muffin praise after each success. A food reward is extremely helpful especially in the initial training. Some dogs love to jump every chance they get.

The Word Pull

The command *pull* requests Muffin to tug or drag something. She probably does this already when she plays with a sock or toy. Linking the word to the tugging action will further enhance your **puppy**'s versatility. She will not only know how to *nose* or push, but she will also know how to *pull*. When you ask Muffin to retrieve an object that is too heavy or too large for her to carry, she might be able to grab it and *pull* it to you. You can even give her a dresser drawer for her toys that she can *pull* out or push closed. Tie a rope to a lever-type door handle, and she can exit the room by pulling on the rope.

To teach the proper response to the *pull* command, find a toy or a sock that Muffin will hold on to and not let you take away easily. Warning: Since puppy's teeth can be damaged by pulling too strenuously, just match your puppy's pulling strength and until she matures a bit, never ask her to pull something too heavy. So, pull only as hard as she pulls, and repeat the word *pull* each time. Many puppies and dogs will growl, so don't be alarmed. It's usually a friendly growl they enjoy making while playing. Try the play session using a 2-foot (.6 m) piece of soft rope. Tie several knots in the rope to help her to grip it. Once you are successful in getting her to *pull* on it, attach the rope to any article that you might want her to *pull*. Over several training sessions slowly reduce the length of the rope by cutting it, until the rope no longer exists, and she pulls on the article itself.

Avoid pulling with Muffin if she tends to be aggressive with people and other dogs. Pulling with you could encourage her to compete for the pack leader job.

The Words Upstairs and Downstairs

If you live in a house with a staircase, you may find it worthwhile to teach Muffin the words *upstairs* and *downstairs.* Once taught, **puppies** can readily associate the command with steps found anywhere. If you are upstairs you may wish to call Muffin from downstairs, or if you are downstairs you may wish to call her from upstairs. You may want to send her to deliver something to someone who is either upstairs or downstairs. If your friends are touring your home and Muffin has caused a pileup at the stairs, a quick command can allow the traffic to continue moving. Your life will benefit from her new knowledge, and her life will be less of a guessing game.

You will be combining two words from Muffin's existing vocabulary with the word *stairs.* When *upstairs* is used, it will direct her to attain a higher level by way of the staircase. When *downstairs* is used, it will direct her to attain the lower level by way of the staircase. You'll find she will make the transition easily. If you and Muffin spend a lot of time hiking, you might find it helpful to add the words *uphill* and *downhill* to her vocabulary.

To teach Muffin the word *stairs,* find a place where she has the option of going both upstairs and downstairs. If there are three levels in your house, the stairways are usually positioned over each other. Begin training between the stairs going up and those going down. Command Muffin to go upstairs. If she starts heading in the wrong direction, say, "No!" Call her to you to try again. If she selects the proper direction and climbs the steps, praise her, and call her back by saying, "Muffin, *come downstairs*." Reward her with a treat and continue the practice. If Muffin stops halfway up or down the steps because she knows you're holding treats, get sneaky yourself. Put a treat on each level above and below you before you select a command. That will get Muffin to run all the way up or down quickly. You should be in fairly good shape yourself after a session of this! Be sure to keep her from heading up or down the wrong stairway, and make sure you use the proper major directive.

With a little repetition and practice, Muffin will learn her new words. As in all the training you've done so far, strive for mastery by trying different staircases, being farther away as you give the command, and having her carry items up and down the stairs.

The Word Stand

The three major positions Muffin can assume are the *sit,* the *down,* and the *stand.* You have already learned about the *sit* and *down* commands in Chapter 8. In the *stand* position, Muffin's body is parallel to the floor, with her weight distributed equally on all four legs. As in the *sit* and *down* commands, once you give the *stand* command, Muffin should assume the position requested and remain motionless until you release her. Though you will not use it as often as you do the *sit* and *down* commands, you will find the *stand* command extremely helpful when you need it. It is convenient to *stand* Muffin if you want to groom or brush her. Often it will be necessary to have her *stand* so that a trick can be learned and accomplished more easily. If she is your traveling companion on wet or muddy days, you can have her *stand* when making a brief stop, instead of her usual *sit.*

To teach Muffin to *stand,* have her *sit* facing you and give the command. Gently lift the rear end of your puppy, positioning her in a *stand* and telling her to *stay.* Reward her with a treat, then tell her to *sit.* Repeat this exercise until the lifting takes only a few fingers under the belly to let her know what you want. Make a big fuss over her the first time that she does a *stand* without help from you. As with all the training you've done, your excitement means everything to her.

The Word Take

Take is a word that will assist you in Muffin's in-house delivery service. When the command is given, Muffin should grab the article you hand her and deliver it to the person you designate. Unlike the *bring* command, in which the person giving the command receives the delivery, *take* is always a delivery of an article to another person. Until now you've had to tell Muffin to hold **the** object and then send her to find the person, saying, "*Go* to **Joey**." The word *take* allows you to give the command in one quick sentence. Just say, "*Go take* it to Joey," as you hand her the article.

The training involved to teach a delivery has been covered earlier in this chapter. Please refer to the training method used to teach Muffin to deliver an article to a particular family member and apply the new terminology to it.

The Command Watch It!

The command *Watch it!* is a handy way of warning Muffin that she should be careful and move out of the way of danger. In general, **puppies** are very trusting animals. They have a hard time learning what they should be afraid of because often they don't get a second chance. They need to make only one mistake to lose their life or to get severely injured. That is why so many puppies and dogs are hit by cars. In a crowd Muffin can easily get stepped on or tripped over. She trusts that no one will harm her, and she's not aware of the fact that some people just won't see her. Muffin will learn from the first few parties that being under a table is a good spot for an observer of her kind.

The command *Watch it!* can be used as a warning and teaching device. When you hike through the woods with Muffin, she may stop in front of you to listen to a strange noise. Unless you are aware of her reaction, you and Muffin may collide. If you've noticed that she has stopped, you can also stop, but make sure you don't give her the *go* command to remove her from your path. If you do, Muffin, hearing your command, might take off after the animal she was listening to and get lost, be injured, or attacked. The proper reaction in this situation is to give the command *Watch it!* with the right emphasis in your voice. Here you are warning Muffin to be more aware and keep out of your way. You should warn her if a

82

car is approaching and quickly show her that the sidewalk is meant for safety. If you are shoveling dirt and Muffin is getting too inquisitive about the smells coming from this mysterious hole, shout, "*Watch it!*" This may scare her away from the hole. A shovel can do much damage to a curious nose.

Avoid stepping over Muffin when she is lying on the floor. If you do step over her, you will be teaching her not to move. She will learn that you and others will always take pains not to step on her. By no means should you trample Muffin! Rather, teach her to get out of your way from the start. Then she'll also get out of other people's way. To train her to get out of the way, pretend that you don't see her and fake a light fall, scolding her to "Watch it!" Inform your house guests of the words to use in case Muffin gets in their way. House guests will generally bend down to her to pet her, or they'll speak baby talk to her to try to get her to move. Neither of these is a highly effective way to correct her.

The training in this book is based on keeping things positive. Don't leave things on a negative note when giving Muffin warnings. Everytime the *Watch it!* command is given, it should be followed with praise for the proper movement. Use *Watch* it! to train your **puppy** to be careful and aware. You'll receive the added benefit of having a **puppy** that will not inconvenience your guests or your family.

As you can see, there are many directions that you can take with Muffin's twenty-word foundation. The future of her language is now up to you. Try to communicate with her as effectively as you can, and you and she will surely be winners.

Parting Words

Don't allow yourself to be overwhelmed by all the material in this book. All it does is outline a good communication system that you can share with your puppy and suggest adjustments in your behavior toward Fluffy so that you will be able to successfully guide and shape her behavior.

Some of you may be quite satisfied with your puppy and her progress after completing the first stages of the training I've suggested. You may feel so satisfied that you will not complete the rest of the program. I encourage you to continue if you can find the time to do so. Those of you who do will find the work exceedingly rewarding, and your puppy will relish in the attention and training you give her.

Though the program seems idealistic, when it is properly followed it will make an obedient puppy out of almost any canine. The reason for this is that the Twenty Magic Words are simple. This simplicity lies in the fact that only nine basic commands need to be taught to give you a most satisfying control over your puppy at home and in public. Once these nine commands are mastered, they can be extended by teaching the secondary commands and the special commands, which will increase your ability to communicate with your puppy. The ten additional words will make Fluffy a real pro. It will give her at least the equivalent of a bachelor's degree in the behavioral sciences from Poopoodo U!

The methods found in this book are based on principles of good training. Reward and encourage any behavior you wish to keep. Make it as easy as you can for your puppy to succeed by progressing one small step at a time. Immediately correct any actions you deem undesirable, and, if possible, turn negatives into positives. Last, be aware of the mistakes you make in communicating with your puppy or in training her. Don't dwell on them and fret over them. Just do your best not to repeat them the next time a similar situation arises.

The teaching of the Twenty Magic Words is easy if the methods I have presented are followed. In the initial training, select a place to hold lessons where there will be a minimum of distraction. When Fluffy masters a command without distractions around her, train her to follow the same command in situations with a gradually increasing number of distractions.

Use food rewards as a training aid in introducing new material and as a form of payment for special deeds accomplished. Rewards such as verbal praise, petting, and playing supply sufficient positive reinforcement in routine situations.

For many centuries, dogs have been the victims of poor handling. Man's and women's best friend has also been the subject of many incorrect notions. One such notion is that you must send your dog to a training school to have an obedient companion. Even if you do, Fluffy's achievements will depend on how well you learn to give commands consistently. It is the same with the training techniques in this book. The book itself will not train your dog. You must do it.

If your dog doesn't obey you, remember that it is your fault, not your dog's. Determine what you are doing wrong. People don't have dumb dogs as opposed to smart dogs. All dogs have the potential to learn. It's just a question of you using the proper training methods. You can't blame owning a problem dog on bad luck. People create problem dogs by not providing the necessary guidance - - the guidance that a dog, like a bright young child, needs.

The old adage "You can't teach an old dog new tricks" compares a person in a rut to an old dog on the false assumption that old dogs can't learn. I'm sure that this adage was not coined by a professional dog trainer. Although training is most effective when begun at an early age, an old dog can easily be taught new lessons.

The dog of mixed breed has been said to be at a disadvantage compared with a purebred dog. Interbreeding is generally thought to be destructive by people who breed dogs. Undoubtedly this is true of the breeds these people are working with and the traits they are trying to develop. Centuries of work have gone into the careful, selective reproduction of most breeds. Indeed, society is fortunate to have such dedicated dog lovers. They breed dogs for specific functions. In each of these specific areas a particular purebred is usually superior to most mixed breeds. However, dogs of mixedbreeds are just as trainable as and sometimes more trainable than purebreds because the mixed breeds may have inherited many of the great instinctual traits found in their different ancestors' genes. They are thus more likely to adapt to a wider range of functions and will often learn faster.

Some people believe that it is unnatural and cruel to train a **puppy** to do anything. This is untrue. It is instinctive for Fluffy to accept training, and she enjoys it. As a puppy she was trained in certain behaviors by her mother. If she had grown up in the wild and joined a pack, she would have had a pack leader or older dogs around her. They would have imparted to her certain behaviors and training. Your training sessions, if carried out according to the advice I have given, will be fun for Fluffy. She will look forward to them, especially if you hold them on a regular basis. Like humans, she loves attention.

Your puppy or dog wants to please you, her master, in every way she can. The only obstacle in her way is poor understanding. Fluffy will do anything within her ability if she understands clearly what you want her to do. The Twenty Magic Words will make it possible for her to understand your commands. They stress good communication methods to increase her knowledge and understanding.

Good communication benefits your **puppy** in many ways. Fluffy will understand more easily what you consider good and bad. Your wishes will be clearer to her, which will satisfy her goal of making you happy and make her life much easier in general. In addition to making your **puppy**'s life happier, it will provide her with added safety and improve her chances for a longer life. You are the one she loves and wants to be with. With good training she will get to spend more time with you, since you will be more inclined to welcome her company and take her with you more often.

The time, the attention, and the love you bestow upon your **puppy** are extremely rewarding investments. Compared with the benefits, the expenses of owning a **puppy** are minimal, both from a financial standpoint and with respect to the expenditure of your time.

There is much satisfaction in pursuing any hobby, but few hobbies can top that of training your dog. In other hobbies you are working with inanimate materials that do not react to you. You may end up with a painting, a piece of needlepoint, a musical score, or a rose garden that may be your pride and joy. But these achievements will not provide warm companionship on a cold night! Like other hobbyists, you can display your handiwork and receive praise and admiration. People are always impressed by a dog that is obedient. They see so few.

In addition to having an enjoyable hobby, training your **puppy** will provide you with therapeutic and psychological benefits. It's mentally healthy for you to have a **puppy** that will always return your affection - - a friend you can count on. The time you spend with your **puppy** will provide a learning experience that can help you in understanding not only your **puppy**, but other people and most importantly - - yourself. Finally, remember that the benefits of giving love, whether to your **puppy** or to a fellow human being, are immeasurable. An

additional dose of love in your life can only increase your happiness.

Everything is up to you now. Your success in teaching the language and using the training methods will assure your puppy's success. Set your goals high and go after them. Allow your puppy to be outstanding in his field and a credit to your work with him. Use the contents of this book as a guideline and refer to the book often. Don't allow it to be a book that sits on your shelf, never to be opened again!

Be sure to subscribe to my YouTube channel. Search "Ted Baer Dog Trainer". I have also written a book with a YouTube channel called "That's Cool!" It offers the perfect opportunity for everyone to raise their cool factor! Learn forty-nine "people" tricks that will impress your friends and dazzle your colleagues! Search "Ted Baer That's Cool".

www.ingramcontent.com/pod-product-compliance
Lightning Source LLC
Chambersburg PA
CBHW060412050426
42449CB00009B/1957